Michelle Gibson
Deborah T. Meem
Editors

Lesbian Academic Couples

Lesbian Academic Couples has been co-published simultaneously as *Journal of Lesbian Studies*, Volume 9, Number 4 2005.

Pre-publication
REVIEWS,
COMMENTARIES,
EVALUATIONS . . .

"The writers gathered here expose the underlying currents that allow them to flourish and continue to grow–opportunity, activism, and great love: for their work, for justice, and for each other."

Chris Cuomo, PhD
Professor of Philosophy
and Women's Studies
University of Cincinnati

More pre-publication
REVIEWS, COMMENTARIES, EVALUATIONS . . .

"Though their title suggests a bland, same-sex melody, Gibson and Meem offer diverse voices that strike dissonant notes and ultimately deliver a jazz performance pulsing with life and possibility. The variety in style and perspective creates a layering effect as each writer disrupts our harmonic notions of home, work, and community. From deans to instructors and from tenured to temporary, these women sing of privilege, longing, literacy, and power. In embodied narratives that defy definition, they describe their fluid sense of place and displacement; some frame their stories in feminist and/or queer theories, and some use a language of transformation that reaches beyond theory into mailrooms, classrooms, and boardrooms where relationships flourish and minds change. Somehow, the collection offers a happy ending, even as it resists closure–a pleasure to hear and hum."

Laura A. Milner, PhD
Assistant Professor
Department of Writing
and Linguistics
Georgia Southern University

"Gibson and Meem offer lesbian academic couples their first scholarly examination. These couples are given a layered look in this anthology that incorporates personal narratives and grounded theoretical analyses. The contributions provide a feminist perspective of this late Capitalist post-Stonewall phenomenon. Topics range from identity negotiation, to reappointment and tenure, to pedagogical interventions, to spousal hiring within academic settings."

Catherine Raissiguier, PhD
Associate Professor of Women's
and Gender Studies
New Jersey City University

"The editors deftly note the ability of these women to live together–economically, socially, emotionally–and expand their careers."

Martha Marinara, PhD
Associate Professor of English
University of Central Florida

Harrington Park Press

Lesbian Academic Couples

Lesbian Academic Couples has been co-published simultaneously as *Journal of Lesbian Studies*, Volume 9, Number 4 2005.

Monographic Separates from the *Journal of Lesbian Studies*

For additional information on these and other Haworth Press titles, including descriptions, tables of contents, reviews, and prices, use the QuickSearch catalog at http://www.HaworthPress.com.

Lesbian Academic Couples, edited by Michelle Gibson and Deborah T. Meem (Vol. 9, No. 4, 2005). *"The writers gathered here expose the underlying currents that allow them to flourish and continue to grow—opportunity, activism, and great love: for their work, for justice, and for each other." (Chris Cuomo, PhD, Professor of Philosophy and Women's Studies, University of Cincinnati)*

Making Lesbians Visible in the Substance Use Field, edited by Elizabeth Ettorre (Vol. 9, No. 3, 2005). *"This is the book that we in the substance abuse treatment and research fields have been waiting for." (Katherine van Wormer, PhD, MSSW, Professor of Social Work, University of Iowa; co-author,* Addiction Treatment: A Strengths Perspective*)*

Lesbian Communities: Festivals, RVs, and the Internet, edited by Esther Rothblum and Penny Sablove (Vol. 9, No. 1/2, 2005). *"Important. . . . Challenging and compelling. . . . A fascinating assortment of diverse perspectives on just what defines a lesbian 'community,' what needs and desires they meet, and how those worlds intersect with other groups and cultures." (Diane Anderson-Minshall, Executive Editor,* Curve *Magazine)*

Lesbian Ex-Lovers: The Really Long-Term Relationships, edited by Jacqueline S. Weinstock and Esther D. Rothblum (Vol. 8, No. 3/4, 2004). *"Compelling. . . . In these heady days of legal gay marriage, this book is a good reminder of the devotion lesbians have always had to the women we've loved, and the vows we've made with our hearts, long before we demanded licenses. This book is a tribute to the long memory we have of the women's hands who have touched our most vulnerable parts, and the invisible hands that outlast our divorces." (Arlene Istar Lev, CSW-R, CSAC, Author of* Transgender Emergence *and* The Complete Lesbian and Gay Parenting Guide*; Founder and Clinical Director, Choices Counseling and Consulting)*

Lesbians, Feminism, and Psychoanalysis: The Second Wave, edited by Judith M. Glassgold and Suzanne Iasenza (Vol. 8, No. 1/2, 2004). *"This book is the first to set the tone for a lesbian psychoanalytic revolution." (Dany Nobus, PhD, Senior Lecturer in Psychology and Psychoanalytic Studies, Brunel University, United Kingdom)*

Trauma, Stress, and Resilence Among Sexual Minority Women: Rising Like the Phoenix, edited by Kimberly F. Balsam, PhD (Vol. 7, No. 4, 2003). *Provides a first-hand look at the victimization experiences that lesbian and bisexual women face as well as how they work through these challenges and emerge resilient.*

Latina Lesbian Writers and Artists, edited by María Dolores Costa, PhD (Vol. 7, No. 3, 2003). *"A fascinating journey through the Latina lesbian experience. It brings us stories of exile, assimilation, and conflict of cultures. The book takes us to the Midwest, New York, Chicana Borderlands, Mexico, Argentina, and Spain. It succeeds at showing the diversity within the Latina lesbian experience through deeply feminist testimonials of life and struggle." (Susana Cook, performance artist and playwright)*

Lesbian Rites: Symbolic Acts and the Power of Community, edited by Ramona Faith Oswald, PhD (Vol. 7, No. 2, 2003). *"Informative, enlightening, and well written . . . illuminates the range of lesbian ritual behavior in a creative and thorough manner. Ramona Faith Oswald and the contributors to this book have done scholars and students of ritual studies an important service by demonstrating the power, pervasiveness, and performative nature of lesbian ritual practices." (Cele Otnes, PhD, Associate Professor, Department of Business Administration, University of Illinois)*

Mental Health Issues for Sexual Minority Women: Redefining Women's Mental Health, edited by Tonda L. Hughes, RN, PhD, FAAN, Carrol Smith, RN, MS, and Alice Dan, PhD (Vol. 7, No. 1, 2003). *A rare look at mental health issues for lesbians and other sexual minority women.*

Addressing Homophobia and Heterosexism on College Campuses, edited by Elizabeth P. Cramer, PhD (Vol. 6, No. 3/4, 2002). *A practical guide to creating LGBT-supportive environments on college campuses.*

Femme/Butch: New Considerations of the Way We Want to Go, edited by Michelle Gibson and Deborah T. Meem (Vol. 6, No. 2, 2002). *"Disrupts the fictions of heterosexual norms. . . . A much-needed examiniation of the ways that butch/femme identitites subvert both heteronormativity and 'expected' lesbian behavior." (Patti Capel Swartz, PhD, Assistant Professor of English, Kent State University)*

Lesbian Love and Relationships, edited by Suzanna M. Rose, PhD (Vol. 6, No. 1, 2002). *"Suzanna Rose's collection of 13 essays is well suited to prompting serious contemplation and discussion about lesbian lives and how they are–or are not–different from others. . . . Interesting and useful for debunking some myths, confirming others, and reaching out into new territories that were previously unexplored." (Lisa Keen, BA, MFA, Senior Political Correspondent, Washington Blade)*

Everyday Mutinies: Funding Lesbian Activism, edited by Nanette K. Gartrell, MD, and Esther D. Rothblum, PhD (Vol. 5, No. 3, 2001). *"Any lesbian who fears she'll never find the money, time, or support for her work can take heart from the resourcefulness and dogged determination of the contributors to this book. Not only do these inspiring stories provide practical tips on making dreams come true, they offer an informal history of lesbian political activism since World War II." (Jane Futcher, MA, Reporter,* Marin Independent Journal, *and author of* Crush, Dream Lover, *and* Promise Not to Tell)

Lesbian Studies in Aotearoa/New Zealand, edited by Alison J. Laurie (Vol. 5, No. 1/2, 2001). *These fascinating studies analyze topics ranging from the gender transgressions of women passing as men in order to work and marry as they wished to the effects of coming out on modern women's health.*

Lesbian Self-Writing: The Embodiment of Experience, edited by Lynda Hall, PhD (Vol. 4, No. 4, 2000). *"Probes the intersection of love for words and love for women. . . . Luminous, erotic, evocative." (Beverly Burch, PhD, psychotherapist and author,* Other Women: Lesbian/Bisexual Experience and Psychoanalytic Views of Women *and* On Intimate Terms: The Psychology of Difference in Lesbian Relationships)

'Romancing the Margins'? Lesbian Writing in the 1990s, edited by Gabriele Griffin, PhD (Vol. 4, No. 2, 2000). *Explores lesbian issues through the mediums of books, movies, and poetry and offers readers critical essays that examine current lesbian writing and discuss how recent movements have tried to remove racist and antigay themes from literature and movies.*

From Nowhere to Everywhere: Lesbian Geographies, edited by Gill Valentine, PhD (Vol. 4, No. 1, 2000). *"A significant and worthy contribution to the ever growing literature on sexuality and space. . . . A politically significant volume representing the first major collection on lesbian geographies. . . . I will make extensive use of this book in my courses on social and cultural geography and sexuality and space." (Jon Binnie, PhD, Lecturer in Human Geography, Liverpool, John Moores University, United Kingdom)*

Lesbians, Levis and Lipstick: The Meaning of Beauty in Our Lives, edited by Jeanine C. Cogan, PhD, and Joanie M. Erickson (Vol. 3, No. 4, 1999). *Explores lesbian beauty norms and the effects these norms have on lesbian women.*

Lesbian Sex Scandals: Sexual Practices, Identities, and Politics, edited by Dawn Atkins, MA (Vol. 3, No. 3, 1999). *"Grounded in material practices, this collection explores confrontation and coincidence among identity politics, 'scandalous' sexual practices, and queer theory and feminism. . . . It expands notions of lesbian identification and lesbian community." (Maria Pramaggiore, PhD, Assistant Professor, Film Studies, North Carolina State University, Raleigh)*

The Lesbian Polyamory Reader: Open Relationships, Non-Monogamy, and Casual Sex, edited by Marcia Munson and Judith P. Stelboum, PhD (Vol. 3, No. 1/2, 1999). *"Offers reasonable, logical, and persuasive explanations for a style of life I had not seriously considered before. . . . A terrific read." (Beverly Todd, Acquisitions Librarian, Estes Park Public Library, Estes Park, Colorado)*

Living "Difference": Lesbian Perspectives on Work and Family Life, edited by Gillian A. Dunne, PhD (Vol. 2, No. 4, 1998). *"A fascinating, groundbreaking collection. . . . Students and professionals in psychiatry, psychology, sociology, and anthropology will find this work extremely useful and thought provoking." (Nanette K. Gartrell, MD, Associate Clinical Professor of Psychiatry, University of California at San Francisco Medical School)*

Lesbian Academic Couples

Michelle Gibson
Deborah T. Meem
Editors

Lesbian Academic Couples has been co-published simultaneously as
Journal of Lesbian Studies, Volume 9, Number 4 2005.

HPP

Harrington Park Press®
An Imprint of The Haworth Press, Inc.

New York • London • Victoria (AU)
www.HaworthPress.com

Published by

Harrington Park Press®, 10 Alice Street, Binghamton, NY 13904-1580 USA

Harrington Park Press® is an imprint of The Haworth Press, Inc., 10 Alice Street, Binghamton, NY 13904-1580 USA.

Lesbian Academic Couples has been co-published simultaneously as *Journal of Lesbian Studies*, Volume 9, Number 4 2005.

Cover design by Kerry E. Mack

Cover image courtesy of Wellesley College Archives.

Library of Congress Cataloging-in-Publication Data

Lesbian academic couples / Michelle Gibson, Deborah T. Meem, editors.
     p. cm.
    Includes bibliographical references and index.
    ISBN-13: 978-1-56023-618-4 (hard cover : alk. paper)
    ISBN-10: 1-56023-618-3 (hard cover : alk. paper)
    ISBN-13: 978-1-56023-619-1 (soft cover : alk. paper)
    ISBN-10: 1-56023-619-1 (soft cover : alk. paper)
    1. Lesbian couples–United States. 2. Lesbian college teachers–United States. I. Gibson, Michelle. II. Meem, Deborah T. (Deborah Townsend), 1949-
HQ75.6.U5L34 2005
306.76'63'0973–dc22
                                              2005011854

Indexing, Abstracting & Website/Internet Coverage

This section provides you with a list of major indexing & abstracting services and other tools for bibliographic access. That is to say, each service began covering this periodical during the year noted in the right column. Most Websites which are listed below have indicated that they will either post, disseminate, compile, archive, cite or alert their own Website users with research-based content from this work. (This list is as current as the copyright date of this publication.)

(continued)

(continued)

Special Bibliographic Notes related to special journal issues (separates) and indexing/abstracting:

- indexing/abstracting services in this list will also cover material in any "separate" that is co-published simultaneously with Haworth's special thematic journal issue or DocuSerial. Indexing/abstracting usually covers material at the article/chapter level.
- monographic co-editions are intended for either non-subscribers or libraries which intend to purchase a second copy for their circulating collections.
- monographic co-editions are reported to all jobbers/wholesalers/approval plans. The source journal is listed as the "series" to assist the prevention of duplicate purchasing in the same manner utilized for books-in-series.
- to facilitate user/access services all indexing/abstracting services are encouraged to utilize the co-indexing entry note indicated at the bottom of the first page of each article/chapter/contribution.
- this is intended to assist a library user of any reference tool (whether print, electronic, online, or CD-ROM) to locate the monographic version if the library has purchased this version but not a subscription to the source journal.
- individual articles/chapters in any Haworth publication are also available through the Haworth Document Delivery Service (HDDS).

ABOUT THE EDITORS

Michelle Gibson is Associate Professor of English and Women's Studies at the University of Cincinnati. She has published poetry and scholarly work in the areas of composition studies and cultural studies, including "The Peculiar Case of Contessa" (*Transformations*, 2004) and co-editing with Jonathan Alexander a special cluster on Queer Theory for *Journal of Advanced Composition* (2004). With Deb Meem she co-edited *Femme/Butch: New Considerations of the Way We Want to Go* (Haworth, 2002).

Deborah T. Meem is Professor of English and Women's Studies at the University of Cincinnati. She has edited Eliza Lynn Linton's novel *The Rebel of the Family* (Broadview, 2002) and published in literary and cultural studies. With Michelle Gibson and Martha Marinara she wrote "Bi, Butch, and Bar Dyke: Pedagogical Performances of Class, Gender, and Sexuality" (*CCC*, 2000), and she and Gibson have collaborated on other articles on butch-femme lesbian gender.

Lesbian Academic Couples

CONTENTS

Margaret Sherwood and Martha Shackford. Wellesley College, early 1900s. Courtesy of Wellesley College Archives.

Introduction

Michelle Gibson
Deborah T. Meem

University of Cincinnati

KEYWORDS. Lesbian, academic couple, Boston Marriage, collaboration

This project began over two years ago. We were in the midst of a shared professional crisis precipitated by our university's restructuring process, which necessitated our being moved to another department in another part of the university. We were unsure of our futures and were thinking seriously about whether we might begin the job search process. We immediately found ourselves listing different possible configura-

---

Michelle Gibson is Associate Professor of English and Women's Studies at the University of Cincinnati. She has published poetry and scholarly work in the areas of composition studies and cultural studies, including "The Peculiar Case of Contessa" (*Transformations*, 2004) and co-editing with Jonathan Alexander a special cluster on Queer Theory for *Journal of Advanced Composition* (2004). With Deb Meem she co-edited *Femme/Butch: New Considerations of the Way We Want to Go* (Haworth, 2002).

Deborah T. Meem is Professor of English and Women's Studies at the University of Cincinnati. She has edited Eliza Lynn Linton's novel *The Rebel of the Family* (Broadview, 2002) and published in literary and cultural studies. With Michelle Gibson and Martha Marinara she wrote "Bi, Butch, and Bar Dyke: Pedagogical Performances of Class, Gender, and Sexuality" (*CCC*, 2000), and she and Gibson have collaborated on other articles on butch-femme lesbian gender.

[Haworth co-indexing entry note]: "Introduction." Gibson, Michelle, and Deborah T. Meem. Co-published simultaneously in *Journal of Lesbian Studies* (Harrington Park Press, an imprint of The Haworth Press, Inc.) Vol. 9, No. 4, 2005, pp. 1-12; and: *Lesbian Academic Couples* (ed: Michelle Gibson, and Deborah T. Meem) Harrington Park Press, an imprint of The Haworth Press, Inc., 2005, pp. 1-12. Single or multiple copies of this article are available for a fee from The Haworth Document Delivery Service [1-800-HAWORTH, 9:00 a.m. - 5:00 p.m. (EST). E-mail address: docdelivery@haworthpress.com].

doi:10.1300/J155v9n04_01

1

tions for our professional lives–both of us working in universities, but living apart from each other; one of us working, the other writing full time; one of us continuing in academe, the other working a professional job outside academe; one of us pursuing an academic position, the other starting her own business; one in a tenure-track academic position, the other working as an adjunct faculty member. The one configuration that seemed nearly impossible to accomplish, though, was the one we had enjoyed since the beginning of our relationship: working together in the same university and in the same department. Neither of us qualified as a famous academic "star" who might seem like such an adornment to another institution that they would hire the partner as a matter of course. So, like many academic couples whose work situations change, we felt like we were facing an inevitable downward trajectory, since it appeared likely that one of us at least would be unable to replicate her present tenured position. And like most lesbian academic couples, we wondered, even if we did happen upon the ideal situation, how long it might take us in a new institution to achieve the level of queer visibility and sense of community we enjoyed in our present positions.

We lucked out. Our new department has treated us with consideration and respect (and a certain benign neglect, which we also appreciate). Part of this treatment is due, we assume, to the fact that we are not the only couple working in the department, although we are the only same-sex couple. Part of this treatment is also due to the culture of English studies as an academic field; it would be shockingly un-hip for an English department faculty member to articulate anti-gay sentiments. At any rate, we have fortunately landed on our feet at our home university, and so could discontinue our job search. The unsettled atmosphere in which we lived for several years motivated us to consider the situation of lesbian academic couples throughout the country, so we sent out a call for papers for this collection.

We were surprised to receive very few responses. Our own experiences as a lesbian academic couple had been fruitful professionally and satisfying personally, and the institutional meltdown we encountered had seemed so arbitrary and so unsettling that we assumed there would be many others like us whose experiences would lead them to analyze their own–and others'–similar situations. But this is not what happened. We did receive a few excellent proposals, but also some which were simple narrations with little or no analysis–in short, not academic writing at all. After circulating a second call for papers which brought us one or two additional promising proposals, we began soliciting articles among our acquaintances. Here again we encountered unexpected negative results. One couple turned us down flat, explaining that they simply could not participate out of concern for maintaining their own privacy. Another couple initially indicated some interest, but did not follow through, presumably because they worried that other faculty at their small college would be compromised by their discussion. In short, while everyone we talked to about the project seemed interested in the subject, few felt ready to contribute materially.

It seemed, as we will discuss later in this introduction, that the authors who finally decided to write for this volume share with us a kind of "immunity"–they are senior faculty with lengthy credentials in LGBT scholarship who have been able to land academic positions not compromised by outing, or junior scholars with a queer specialty, or established academicians who have been outed and whose lesbianism had already been used against them, or mobile academics willing to use their constantly shifting and unpredictable work lives as grist for this mill.

LESBIAN ACADEMIC COUPLES:
TODAY'S WELLESLEY MARRIAGES?

Lillian Faderman describes a Boston marriage as "a long-term monogamous relationship between two otherwise unmarried women" (*Surpassing* 190) in the late nineteenth and early twentieth centuries. A "Wellesley marriage" specifically referred to female academic couples. Patricia Palmieri, writing about the first generations of faculty at Wellesley College (in the 1870s and after), describes a community of "women-committed women" (xv) who formed "[l]ifelong friendships of deep significance," a group of "educated spinsters renouncing marriage in favor of intimacy and support from other women" (137). Indeed, for those pioneers in higher education for women, marriage to a man was simply out of the question if they wished to remain professors. Even progressive men assumed as a matter of course that a woman morphed into a homebody immediately upon marriage. For example, George Herbert Palmer, who supported women's rights in general and youthful Alice Freeman's work as president of Wellesley in particular, and who protested "of course I had no idea of closing her career" (176), coerced Freeman into resigning from the presidency when she married him; he wrote with considerable self-congratulation that the "shelter of a home had enlarged her scope" (221). Part of the design of Wellesley marriages was to create alternative families, and in so doing permit academic women to continue in their chosen careers.

These early female academic couples illustrate a phenomenon that was peculiar to the period 1870-1920–that long-term partnerships between women were seen as neither unnatural nor immoral, and therefore that they could be treated with the kind of openness and respect characteristic of married heterosexual couples. This was true in the academy, at Wellesley and elsewhere, and decidedly did not prevent the individuals from gaining fame and prestige. Katharine Lee Bates, professor of English at Wellesley and author of "America the Beautiful," lived with Katharine Coman, chair of Wellesley's Economics Department and Dean of the College, for 25 years. After Coman's death in 1915, Bates could write, "So much of me died with Katharine Coman that I'm sometimes not sure whether I'm alive or not" (Palmieri 139). She could also publish a volume of poetry, *Yellow Clover*, dedicated to her life with Coman. Similarly, Bryn Mawr College president M. Carey Thomas lived openly on campus with her companion Mamie Gwinn until Gwinn married in 1904, and then with Mary Garrett until Garrett's death in 1915. According to Thomas's biographer Helen Lefkowitz Horowitz, Thomas was not only open about living in a "Wellesley marriage," but also acknowledged the possibility of physical love between women; at the same time Thomas was an internationally known authority on women's higher education.

Partnerships between women were also commonplace outside the academy during this period, and were often treated with matter-of-fact respect and courtesy. Molly Dewson, well-known New Deal Democratic politico, lived with Polly Porter for 52 years, and could demand that she work out of New York rather than Washington, DC, in order to be near her beloved "Partner" (Ware 128). Better known today are long-time couple Gertrude Stein and Alice B. Toklas, who lived together from 1907 until Stein's death in 1946. Their open relationship may have elicited some laughter and snide remarks, but it never prevented famous artists and writers from vying to be seen at their salon. Another well-known couple was Jane Addams and Mary Rozet Smith. Addams founded Hull House in Chicago together with her first partner Ellen Starr, then later lived with Smith for over thirty years. These female couples, both inside and outside of academia, enjoyed a kind of social acceptance born of the assumption that women who did not marry men might logically form lasting relationships with women.

In discussing these early female partnerships, we have profiled only white women, thereby following the prevailing notion that the "Boston marriage" phenomenon was restricted to white, middle- or upper-class, often college educated women. Certainly Black women of the same period had far less access to education and to publishing venues, and so were unlikely to become widely known *as* couples. It is beginning to become apparent, however, that some Black women did establish and maintain long-term romantic friendships of this type. Recent research by Farah Jasmine Griffin has brought forth the letters between domestic servant Addie Brown and teacher of freed slaves Rebecca Primus in the years immediately following the Civil War. Stacey Robertson feels that the

> Brown-Primus relationship also challenges our understanding of White women's sexuality in the nineteenth century. Although Griffin does not discuss this at length, I would suggest that Brown and Primus' relationship reflects the "Boston marriages" that emerged a bit later in the century. Historians have seen the Boston marriage as an intimate relationship between middle- or upper-class, educated, white women. The Brown-Primus letters demand that we rethink our assumptions about such relationships–making more effort to look beyond the limited scope of White middle-class college women. (Robertson)

Should we think of those women as lesbians? Scholars are divided on this point. Blanche Wiesen Cook weighs in on the side of assuming a continuity of lesbian experience, and is content to classify nineteenth-century romantic friendships as lesbian relationships. Most contemporary critics are less willing to apply the term "lesbian" to women who did not have that word to describe themselves. Faderman, for instance, assumes that "lesbian identity . . . is peculiar to the twentieth century and owes its start at least partly to those sexologists who attempted to separate off women who continued to love other women from the rest of humankind" (*Odd Girls* 4). To be sure, the sexologists–all male, all interested in the grand taxonomic project of sorting out every type of human behavior and personality–had an agenda to promote: restraint of freedom-seeking women. Their invention of categories of sexual inversion pathologized lesbianism, and ultimately had the effect of ending the benign "Wellesley marriage" era. After roughly 1920 (the "Fall" from pre-World War I innocence, according to Nancy Sahli), two women making a home together were at least suspected of deviant behavior, and perhaps also assumed to embody the newly named identity "lesbian." Since that time, a lesbian academic couple has been taken to have a sexual as well as a scholarly element.

Fall or no fall, however, we see a definite historical linkage between today's lesbian academic couples and our predecessors from a century and more ago. We recognize them as ancestors, and feel sure they would recognize us as well; we, like they, comprise a pair of academics, committed to our profession, and at the same time part of an emotional and economic dyad that orders our lives. As examples, let us focus briefly on two early couples, Mary Woolley and Jeannette Marks from Mt. Holyoke College, and Margaret Sherwood and Martha Shackford of Wellesley College. Woolley and Marks in fact met at Wellesley; Woolley was a professor of Biblical history and Marks was a student. Woolley moved to Mt. Holyoke when she was offered the presidency there; Marks followed a year later, and taught English. Mary Woolley earned considerable fame in her life, and during the first decade of their relationship Marks seems to have experienced some discomfort at her own comparative eclipse. Nevertheless, Marks became head of the English Department at Mt. Holyoke and was a prolific scholar. The two women were together as a couple for 52 years. Sherwood and Shackford also met at Wellesley, where Sherwood was a professor of English and Shackford was a student. There seems to be no question that sparks flew between the two women; "Students gossiped that Miss Shackford stole Miss Sherwood from Miss Jewett" (Palmieri 137). Eleven years older, Sherwood supported Shackford's career; eventually Shackford earned her doctorate at Yale and returned to Wellesley's English Department.

Concerned that women students involved in intense emotional relationships with one another were distracted from their academic work by the melodrama inherent in such relationships, Marks wrote an essay–"Unwise College Friendships"–in which she characterized relationships between women as "unpleasant or worse," "abnormal," and sicknesses that should be eliminated with "moral antiseptic" (Faderman, *Surpassing* 229). Though Marks was clearly concerned with love between female students and perhaps not even considering her relationship with Woolley to be equivalent, it is (as Faderman notes) clear that Marks had internalized a kind of distaste for relationships very much in the same vein as her own. What a difference a hundred years makes! Now two lesbian academics (for example, the two of us, Verta Taylor and Leila Rupp, and many others) involved in a loving relationship with one another might well work together on projects with the word *lesbian* in the title. They might enjoy a kind of acceptance as a couple from their colleagues, and they might even be known to their LGBT students as a couple who can be approached for support and advice.

In our own situation, colleagues and students alike treat us as they might any other couple–with a few unexpected differences. First, queer students seem to us much more likely to be positively predisposed to like us. They seek us out, coming to our offices with the assumption that we will be available for conversation about their personal lives–problems or joys in romantic relationships, trouble with families who are judgmental or who reject them altogether, and difficulties with friends or authority figures. Second, our colleagues seem to go out of their way to let us know that they respect our relationship and value our individual and shared contributions to the department. Finally, and perhaps most significant, one difference between our situation and that of our heterosexually married colleagues is that our identity as a lesbian academic couple earns us a kind of political and professional capital.

Our scholarly collaborations have been extraordinarily fruitful. Within our first year as a couple we published an article about butch/femme identity and its impact on our students' "readings" of us as instructors. Later, we worked with a third colleague to publish an article about the impact of instructors' gender, sexual preference, and social class on their students' interactions with them. In 2002 our special issue of *Journal of Lesbian Studies* devoted to the examination of Butch/Femme lesbian gender appeared. Presently, we are working on this volume and on another (unrelated) book-length project. Not once since we have begun collaborating has anyone questioned the value of academic discussions of issues related to lesbianism. In fact, aside from one "moment" in our career when someone questioned the notion that collaboration itself has value, we can say without any hesitation that our institution has been an extraordinarily welcoming professional home for us as a lesbian academic couple.

Working on this project has brought home to us (not for the first time, to be sure) that our situation, though shared by some, simply does not obtain for many other lesbian academic couples in this country. Perhaps even more troubling, there seems to be a move toward what we call a "conservative retrenchment," a backlash by conservatives against the progress made by liberals and leftists over the past 30 years. This phenomenon has resulted in a number of disturbing developments both at the legislative and at the personal level. In November 2004, thirteen states, including our own (Ohio) passed anti-gay defense of marriage acts. Indeed, "[l]egal experts have called Ohio's ban the broadest of 13 state amendments passed this year because it forbids any legal status 'that intends to approximate the design, qualities, significance or effect of marriage'" ("Ohio's Marriage Amendment"). This seems to mean, although dozens of lawsuits are pending, that civil unions and domestic partner benefits, not to mention enforcement of domestic violence statutes and the rights of unmarried older couples, will also be jeopardized. In addition, the right-wing organization Focus on the Family and their allies have launched a number of campaigns against companies like Disney and Procter and Gamble because of what they perceive as pro-gay policies (Crary, Vitagliano).

We mention this conservative backlash partly to highlight the current dicey political climate around LGBT issues, but mostly to emphasize our own privilege of safety within our institution. Part of that safety is our privilege of writing this book, and knowing that not only are we immune to firing or censorship or intimidation for bringing up the subject, but the book will "count" in terms of the scholarly expectations in our department. We know anecdotally that many other lesbian academic couples do not enjoy the same privilege, and thus have been reluctant to participate in this project. Colleagues we talk to at conferences tell us that they are encouraged (read ordered) not to be out as queers on campus, and that they are discouraged (read forbidden) from doing academic work in the area of LGBT studies. As we said, our own institution has in so many ways been extremely supportive of queer curricula and scholarship, and there is an active, engaged, and nationally recognized queer community. Nonetheless, a former dean of the unit in which we taught for years once challenged the introduction into our curriculum of an LGBT literature course by questioning its "validity" and importance to a liberal arts curriculum. In short, change for the better has occurred in pockets and most often even within those pockets there are those who continue to resist it. Our national conversations about what LGBT or queer scholarship should focus on are almost always impacted by our differing circumstances. Those living and working within politically progressive pockets see us moving forward, beyond questions of equality and inclusion; those who live outside these pockets understand that the need for such conversations has not been eradicated–and that in many ways their own lives depend on them. What this means is that almost any discussion around issues of sexuality that we have at this moment is simultaneously before its time, in its time, and long overdue–and that is an odd place in which to work. It's an even odder place in which to collaborate with lesbian scholars who live in other parts of the country, which is what editors undertake to do when they initiate a project like this one.

It can't be accidental, then, that there has been almost no scholarship on lesbian academic couples (in the present day; as stated above, there

3

has been some scholarly consideration of Wellesley marriages from a century or more ago). Marianne Ferber and Jane Loeb's 1997 collection *Academic Couples: Problems and Promises* includes a single article about unmarried academic couples (Miller and Skeen). *The Chronicle of Higher Education* has offered many articles on academic couples, but few that consider the situation of same-sex couples (Risner); a notable exception is the case of Shelli Fowler and Karen DePauw at Virginia Tech, discussed in their article in this collection. To be sure, the *Chronicle* has published pieces dealing with (generic, i.e., normally heterosexual) couples whose conclusions also pertain to same-sex couples (Wilson), but the particular conditions faced by LGBT couples in academia are elided in such articles. Graduate student online publications have raised the subject of same-sex dual career couples ("Dilemma"), but the combination of female and lesbian partnerships has not been stressed. We have to conclude that these few articles, together with those contained in this collection, represent merely the tip of a sizeable hidden iceberg of experiences and voices that remain below the radar.

The first article included here is Rachel Morley's "a stitch in time: an experiment in collaboration." In this piece Morley explores what might be called an expanded definition of what an academic couple is. She focuses on nineteenth century collaborators Katharine Bradley and Edith Cooper, an aunt and niece who lived together in a romantic relationship, and who wrote together under the pen name "Michael Field." Morley also includes insights and opinions from contemporary critics Michel Foucault, Germaine Greer, and Luce Irigaray, whom she invites into a "conversation" with Bradley and Cooper. Morley thus constructs a piece of "cut-up writing" that allows the other five individuals to at once "belong to" her, and "to say something about the erotic sensation of academic textual play" (16).

Verta Taylor and Leila Rupp, well known for their contributions to lesbian scholarship over the last quarter century, offer us their story as a longtime academic couple. Their dual memoir, "Becoming the 'Professors of Lesbian Love,'" traces their intertwining personal and professional lives, focusing on the high points, the traumatic low points, and many of the confusing and tension-producing situations that fall in between. Theirs is a story of triumph–one of those rare narratives that end not in separation or silencing, but in scholarly success and reaffirmed relationship.

By contrast, Mary Stuck and Mary Ware tell a story not of victorious togetherness, but enforced separation. Their article "We're Both Tenured Professors . . . but Where Is Home?" examines a common life tra-

jectory: a dual-career academic couple separated when they are unable
to find two viable positions in the same geographical area. Though this
is a familiar enough story to readers of *The Chronicle of Higher Education*
and is even highlighted in Ferber and Loeb's book, the lesbian version
has, as far as we know, simply not been told in a public setting until
now.

While Stuck and Ware describe sacrificing significant relationship
elements to allow both to pursue successful careers, Patricia Lengermann
and Jill Niebrugge tell of their choice to abandon the security of
tenured positions apart for the "world well lost" together. In "'Course is
Team Taught': Dimensions of Difference in Classroom Pedagogy" they
undertake a fascinating project: they interweave their story as a mixed-
race, professionally marginalized (through living on a combination of
temporary, visiting, and adjunct teaching positions) couple with an in-
sightful analysis of key ways in which they embody a pedagogical
challenge to the students they team teach.

On one level, "Dual-Career Queer Couple Hiring in Southwest Virginia: Or, the Contract That Was Not One" tells the story of a fraught but
finally successful spousal hire of a lesbian academic couple at Virginia
Tech. But it is much more than a tale of difficulties resolved in a happy
ending. It shows that prestige and level of administrative position do not
create safety for queers in academia. As Shelli Fowler and Karen
DePauw reveal, one homophobic remark and an institution is running
scared, even one that has a sexual orientation nondiscrimination policy in
place. State universities are often at the mercy of appointed (read rich and
conservative) Boards of Visitors, Boards of Trustees, or Boards of Re-
gents that can exercise a frightening degree of power over decisions that
ought rightly to be made by university administrators and/or faculty.

Chantal Nadeau takes a diametrically opposed position. Her essay
"Unruly Democracy and the Privileges of Public Intimacy: (Same) Sex
Spousal Hiring in Academia" argues that the practice of spousal hiring
by its very nature supports a kind of sexist and heterosexist paradigm in
which the committed monogamous romantic relationship is privileged
over any other kind of relationship. What's more, it encourages queers
to pursue accommodationist activism, seeking, for example, state sanc-
tioning through marriage, domestic partner benefits, or spousal hiring
package plans.

Finally, our article "Performing Transformation: Reflections of a
Lesbian Academic Couple" considers the issues of queerness and privilege as they intermingle in our own story of living out as a lesbian academic couple. Theorizing from experience, we examine how pushing

toward a constantly contested queer space can lead us–and our queer and straight colleagues–to a kind of literacy, power, and transformation based on a choice to live on the other side of the closet.

We think this collection constitutes a fairly dramatic first step in examining the lives of lesbian academic couples. The importance of such an examination is that it encourages us to theorize from the most basic level, namely our own lives. The critique often leveled at academics in general–of course including queer academics–is that our scholarly work is esoteric and not applicable to the day-to-day lived experiences of "real people" in the "real world." To some degree this is an accurate critique; after all, why sully a perfect theory by placing it in the imperfect sphere of experience? On the other hand, scholars, particularly lesbian and feminist scholars, have shown an extraordinary ability to "dive into the wreck" and emerge with clearer and more acute vision. The scholars who have contributed to this project have, we think, done the difficult and often breathtaking work of submerging themselves in experience, exploring it, and reemerging theoretically enriched.

REFERENCES

Addams, Jane. *Twenty Years at Hull House.* NY: Macmillan, 1912. Available at *http:// digital.library.upenn.edu/women/addams/hullhouse/hullhouse.html.*

Cook, Blanche Wiesen. "Women Alone Stir My Imagination: Lesbianism and the Cultural Tradition." *Signs* 4 (Summer 1979): 718-40.

Crary, David. "P & G Faces Conservative Boycott." *Cincinnati Post* 29 October 2004. *http://www.cincypost.com/2004/10/29/pgboycott102904.html.*

"The Dilemma of Dual Career Couples in Academia." *Gradvoice Online.* Available at *http://www.ags.uci.edu/gradvoice/97spring/couple.html.*

Faderman, Lillian. *Odd Girls and Twilight Lovers: A History of Lesbian Life in Twentieth-Century America.* Harmondsworth: Penguin, 1991.

_____. *Surpassing the Love of Men: Romantic Friendship and Love Between Women from the Renaissance to the Present.* NY: William Morrow, 1981.

Ferber, Marianne, and Jane Loeb, eds. *Academic Couples: Problems and Promises.* Urbana and Chicago: U of Illinois P, 1997.

Griffin, Farah Jasmine, ed. *Beloved Sisters and Loving Friends: Letters of Rebecca Primus of Royal Oak, Maryland, and Addie Brown of Hartford, Connecticut, 1854-1868.* NY: Knopf, 1999.

Horowitz, Helen Lefkowitz. *The Power and Passion of M. Carey Thomas.* NY: Knopf, 1994.

Koymasky, Matt and Andrej. "Jane Addams." *The Living Room: Biographies. http:// andrejkoymasky.com/liv/fam/bioa1/adda1.html.*

Miller, Dorothy C. and Anita Skeen. "POSSLQs and PSSSLQs: Unmarried Academic Couples." In *Academic Couples: Problems and Promises*. Marianne Ferber and Jane Loeb, Eds. Urbana and Chicago: U of Illinois P, 1997. 106-127.

Palmer, George Herbert. *The Life of Alice Freeman Palmer*. Boston and NY: Houghton Mifflin, 1908.

Palmieri, Patricia. *In Adamless Eden: The Community of Women Faculty at Wellesley*. New Haven: Yale UP, 1995.

Relyea, Neil. "Ohio's Marriage Amendment Goes In Effect Thursday." 22 January 2005. *http://www.wcpo.com/news/2004/local/12/01/marriage_amendment.html*.

Risner, Doug. "Two Men and a Teenager: Career Considerations of a Same-Sex Couple." *The Chronicle of Higher Education* (5/18/01). Available at *http://chronicle.com/jobs/2001/05/2001051803c.htm*.

Robertson, Stacey. Review of *Beloved Sisters and Loving Friends: Letters of Rebecca Primus of Royal Oak, Maryland, and Addie Brown of Hartford, Connecticut, 1854-1868*. Ed. Farah Jasmine Griffin. Available at *http://w5.usc.edu:9673/review/iglr/review.html?rec_id=513*.

Sahli, Nancy. "Smashing: Women's Relationships Before the Fall," *Chrysalis* 6 (1979): 17-27.

Vitagliano, Ed. "Children's TV Unites to Launch Pro-Homosexual Campaign of 'Tolerance.'" *AFAOnline* (American Family Association). 10 January 2005. *http://headlines.agapepress.org/archive/1/afa/102005a.asp*.

Ware, Susan. *Partner and I: Molly Dewson, Feminism, and New Deal Politics*. New Haven and London: Yale UP, 1987.

Wilson, Robin. "Study of Couples in Academe Finds Least Stress When Both Spouses Work at Same College." *The Chronicle of Higher Education* (7/23/02). *http://chronicle.com/daily/2002/07/2002072301n.htm*.

a stitch in time:
an experiment in collaboration

Rachel Morley

Macquarie University, Sydney

SUMMARY. Writing biography is rarely as straightforward as simply drawing together the threads of someone else's life. Not only must the biographer grapple with the challenge of pulling that life into a narrative shape, she must also deal with the issue of the biographical self to consider the way in which that self impacts and influences the story. Seen like this, biography becomes a collaborative experience–a mesh of self/other relations. Using the case study of the "Michael Fields "–the subjects of my biography in-progress–this paper explores the effects of the researcher/ subject relationship and the way in which it effects a kind of scholarly desire both on (and off) the page. *[Article copies available for a fee from The Haworth Document Delivery Service: 1-800-HAWORTH. E-mail address: <docdelivery@haworthpress.com> Website: <http://www.HaworthPress.com> © 2005 by The Haworth Press, Inc. All rights reserved.]*

Rachel Morley, a former journalist, is now a doctoral candidate at Macquarie University (Sydney), where she is writing a creative/critical thesis that deals with her obsession with the Michael Fields. She has published papers on a diverse range of topics including biography and autobiography, the Helen Demidenko controversy, the Michael Fields, and Australian women's boxing.

[Haworth co-indexing entry note]: "a stitch in time: an experiment in collaboration." Morley, Rachel. Co-published simultaneously in *Journal of Lesbian Studies* (Harrington Park Press, an imprint of The Haworth Press, Inc.) Vol. 9, No. 4, 2005, pp. 13-24; and: *Lesbian Academic Couples* (ed: Michelle Gibson, and Deborah T. Meem) Harrington Park Press, an imprint of The Haworth Press, Inc., 2005, pp. 13-24. Single or multiple copies of this article are available for a fee from The Haworth Document Delivery Service [1-800-HAWORTH, 9:00 a.m. - 5:00 p.m. (EST). E-mail address: docdelivery@haworthpress.com].

Available online at http://www.haworthpress.com/web/JLS
© 2005 by The Haworth Press, Inc. All rights reserved.
doi:10.1300/J155v9n04_02

KEYWORDS. Lesbian, academic couple, Michael Field, Katharine Bradley, Edith Cooper, collaboration

COLLABORATION

Then the old poet began a tale. The first exercise of the free woman is to devise her own mode of revolt, a mode which will reflect her own independence and originality.

Of course we dared not talk much betraying talk. We must remember we are Michael Field. We are hated, as Shelley was hated, by our countrymen, blindly, ravenously. We clasp each other with an awful weight of anxiety on our hearts, for they may strive to part us. We have many things to say that the world will not tolerate from a woman's lips.

We are closer married . . . Yes. Two days after thou wert gone, bleeding came–God's quiet sign that I must open my secret. When it came out the flesh seemed to remember its own self–it was so wakeful; it had been dreaming.

A fatal kiss. There is the silence, the sense of flight to far corners, that one feels in a house before a coffin is brought out. Women's sexual organs are always shrouded in mystery. Liberty is terrifying but it is also exhilarating . . .

My Aunt and I work together after the fashion of Beaumont and Fletcher. Growing closer and closer in spirit. Sexuality was carefully confined; it moved into the home. On the subject of sex, silence became the rule. The problem of "speaking (as) woman" is precisely that of finding a possible continuity between that gestural expression or that speech of desire–which at present can only be identified in the form of symptoms and pathology–and a language, including a verbal language.

Some of the scenes of our play are like mosaic work–the mingled various product of our two brains. If two individuals of exactly the same nature are joined together, they make up a single individual, doubly stronger than each other alone. Edith and I make a *veritable Michael.*

What led us to show, ostentatiously, that sex is something we hide, to say it is something we silence? Well, you are a seedy lot. The revolutionary woman must know her enemies, the doctors, psychiatrists, health visitors, priests, marriage counselors, policemen, magistrates and genteel reformers. What is at issue, briefly, is the over-all "discursive fact," the way in which sex is "put into discourse."

Who does the love scenes?

Listen you tragic dramatists! We shall never "speak out" . . . There is the silence . . .

I have a sense of an invalid in a yellow gown passing along cold stone passages, prison-like in aspect, and then being set down in a room, an insolent, dark-bearded man at a desk.

"Such learned, clever ladies–and they write . . . ?"

When he heard we were aunt and niece, he exclaimed, "It is more like a fairy tale than ever."

Why am I denied what I was made for? What paths have brought us to the point where we are "at fault" with respect to our own sex? The Gods learn little from the stupid words addressed to them at their shrines. There have always been women who rebelled against their role in society. A new poem was evolved before us, that only wanted writing. Just the consummation of ideal passion. There may be a speaking-among-women that is still speaking (as) man but that may also be the place where a speaking (as) woman may dare to express itself. You are destroying this philosophic truth. You are robbing us of real criticism.

I am sorry I should have to explain this to you. But then, you see, I am a woman, and to bring out a play is experience of life–just what women feel so crushingly that they need. You see, Father, I am an artist to the fingertips and I must bring the whole of my life to art, express it in terms of art. You men get it like breathing.

I am filled with jealousy.

I have almost lost consciousness.

"No," says Michael, "I'll not pass those dogs till they are chained."

O Monsieur, on ne craint pas quand on aime. Everything happens as in a dream and to someone I watch. I create phantasies that come so fast that they form an element round me in which I sink, sink–then float along under them and then sink again. We make a vow, which neither speaks, that nothing but death shall sever us. She has lived with me, taught me, encouraged me and joined me to her poetic life. Delirium is glorious, like being inspired continuously. Every moment is plastic. I dance at balls, I go to Operas, I am Mars and, looking across at Sim's little bed, I realize that she is a goddess, hidden in her hair–Venus.

Then I see our two straight beds–they are coffins–we lie near one another in noble peace. Yet I cannot reach her. She is under the possession of a terrible fleshly love. All is gone from that treacherous white sand–Memory. The fear of death makes me cold, but the thought of losing my life on earth with my beloved, brings warmth and tears.

I–I have no tears.

You are beginning where I am leaving off. Your belief in us will go on. Repetition is born of Encouragement. This time I send you a book–partly mine. This happy union of two in work and aspiration is sheltered and expressed by "Michael Field." Please regard him as the author. If you taste the fruit, it will not have been grown in vain. For the rest of our lives can be but sequels–the big volume is closed. I return a poet and possessing a Poet. This book represents only another contribution to a continuing dialogue between the wondering woman and the world.

It is Paradise between us.

CORROBORATION

There is a pleasure in touching bodies. A writing body is no different. In a book–a textual world of sorts–it is not simply the words that matter, those words that appear on the page, glyphs that look like these; it is the spaces in between, the crackle of fissured heat. For books are more than a series of dots and dashes and curls across pages; they are sensory objects, which, like their reader–indeed like their author–recoil or extend to the touch. They emit an invitation for an intimacy of sorts, for silently shared moments between reader, story and writer. Covers are slipped between, pages flutter, only to be unfurled, turned and traversed, giving way to a fleeting passage of time where reality blurs with imagination and the world–briefly–is no longer what it was.

The first part of this writing is a collaboration; it is a cut-up, a collage of voices staged between three contemporary academics–Michel Foucault,[1] Germaine Greer[2] and Luce Irigaray[3]–and two (in)famous nineteenth century collaborators, Katharine Bradley and Edith Cooper,[4] an aunt and niece who lived together, loved together, and wrote together under the pen name of "Michael Field."[5] Drawing on the Dadaist and the Surrealist practices of Tristian Tzara, Brion Gysin and William S. Burroughs, the piece pierces the physicality of each of the four texts in order to re-member writing's construction and the deliberate Borgesian act of writing the present through the continuum of texts that make up the past. As with any cut-up writing, none of the words are mine, yet shredded line by line, piece by piece, and then sewn back together in an order that is entirely of my own making, they all, each of them, belong to me and they all, each of them, aim to say something about the erotic sensation of academic textual play. For, as a woman making-sense of the lives of two loving women under the auspices of biography and within the scholarly realm more broadly, I find myself submerged in the most sensual of stories.

In cut-up writing meanings produced evolve through chance, while the reader's knowledge of the now-ghostly[6] context continues to shroud each line so that the final text is a coordinated choreography that dances between Katharine and Edith and contemporary theoretical ideas and concepts to show how critics–at least this one–participate in reconstructing historical subjects through the politics of the present to produce what may be termed an "(un)conscious collaborative biography," an academic exchange marked out by past/present desires where the line between self and other can be as blurred as the collaboration itself.

Like the collaborator and the cut-up artist, the biographer takes textual fragments bequeathed to her by her subjects and blends them (un)consciously with her own experiential participation in culture, to re-order and remake the body that walks and talks. The biography, like the collaboration, meshes together a coterie of voices to produce a narrative comprised of an in/visible self-other psychic and physical dual-representation–that of the writer and of her subject. For what else is biography if not a cut-up of texts and ideas stemming from "others," rearranged for contemporary consumption according to the writer's own whims and fancies? As Harold Nicolson observed in 1946: "Biography is always a collaboration between the author and his subject; always there must be the reflection of one temperament in the mirror of the other . . ."[7]

Cut-up writing is like collaboration is like biography. It is continuous. The idea of one voice is suspended and the writing shifts, passing between the membranous textures that separate "self" and "other," "real" and "imagined," and the "known" and the "unknown" to create new texts and new meanings. Each brings into question issues concerning creativity and the source point of origin to ask "where does writing come from and what (or whom) informs writing practice?"

This cut-up deliberately juxtaposes fragments from Katharine and Edith's jointly written diary–edited and selected by T.D. and D.C. Sturge Moore and published under the title *Works and Days* (1933)–alongside the academic theorists who are helping to shape my biographical re-visioning of the pair as part of a bid to create new positions from which to speak about "Michael Field" and the performance of collaboration more broadly. I have selected Sturge Moore's text, rather than citing the original journals held in the British Library, because it is Sturge Moore's edition which forms the primary resource for contemporary theorists seeking to trace the couple's biographical roots. They collaborate with him in order to create.

Germaine Greer's *The Female Eunuch* (1971) has had a major impact on my own self-understanding as well as my broader feminist education ever since my mother pressed it into my hands at the age of twelve. Greer taught me that women must rebel, that "[t]he first exercise of the free woman is to devise her own mode of revolt, a mode which will reflect her own independence and originality."[8] No feminist or cultural theorist can escape Michel Foucault's *The History of Sexuality* (1984), while Luce Irigaray has proven inspirational in her "speculative" discourses on the text-uality of women.

I see all of these texts as quiet collaborators in my own writing, "writing ceaselessly" my readings of Edith and Katharine who, in turn, read and write me. Our writings, despite the separation born out of life and of death, are recursive. We speak to each other as wondering academic women opening up a dialogue with the world.[9]

Yet, as Edith Cooper and Katharine Bradley revealed through their own practices, lesbian collaborative writing takes the politics of collaboration further. This is particularly true for those pre-twentieth century women involved in a collaborative poetics aimed at surpassing the "burden" of femaleness and at bypassing the masculinist traditions that muted women's creative productions. Not only do they confront the conventional idea that creativity is a unitary, solitary and usually male production, thus inscribing a new writing praxis by challenging patriarchal stereotypes, they also bring to account the once-shadowy terrain of shared intimacies between women, inventing new speaking roles and creating what Whitney Chadwick and Isabelle de Courtivron term "multiple definitions of creativity."[10] In *Significant Others* (1993), an edited collection of essays on collaborative writing by lovers, Chadwick and de Courtivron write that collaboration beyond heterosexuality pushes new boundaries to open up both discursive and subjective possibilities:

> The realities of artistic partnership also include domestic arrangements which are not bound by the model of heterosexual unions. Here the complexities, and the possibilities for rethinking notions of partnership and of creativity, are even more challenging in that gendered roles are often blurred, and the partners are called upon to reinvent, to refigure the myths into new realities.[11]

Lesbian collaborative writing then provides both personal and creative sanctuary as well as a combined political voice with which to speak. It is both exploratory and (re)visionary, (re)productive and (re)constructive, a (re)telling of the past through new narrative eyes. Writing my portrait of Katharine and Edith, I feel like I am engaging in a triptych collaboration. We are hinged together–through our love of writing, of (re)writing, and our shared commitment for a feminist, lesbian writing praxis: we are each (re)visionists, (re)writing myths to produce "new realities"; they in their (re)writings of Sappho, of Queen Mary, me in my (re)writing of them. I want to rescue them from erasure, from those who seek to divide them, to de-sexualize them, to refine them. I want to help them to speak what I hear.

And yet, like any collaborative praxis, this writing is dangerous. Certainly it is not always harmonious. For as I write my portrait of Katharine and Edith I cannot help but be aware of the way in which I am (un)consciously working both with and against them in accordance with the influences harking back to my own theoretical and subjective positioning to produce a very particular biographical account. In writing them I must continually ask myself at what point do I, still searching for my own intellectual place, my own personal place, bleed into the lives I am trying to represent, creating an on/off-page scholarly partnership with the subjects I study? Like the collaborator who looks at the final "seamless" work she has constructed in liaison with her partner, unable to determine "who wrote what,"[12] where do I stop and they begin? Who are they and where am I? Or, where are they and who am I?

Of interest to most academics, including myself, is the exact nature of their relationship. Did they "collaborate" both intellectually and sexually? Were they lovers in the physical sense? While Sturge Moore does not commit to answering this question, their first biographer, Mary Sturgeon, was quick to assert that there was nothing "abnormal" about their bond.[13] Certainly contemporary biographers and critics, under the more liberating influence of the political and cultural present, claim them as having enjoyed a physical relationship, what we would now call lesbian. Indeed the lines that I have incorporated into my cut-up "[w]e *are closer married*"[14] and "[s]he has lived with me, taught me, encouraged me and joined me to her poetic life"[15] have each been interpreted through an Irigarian polemic as voicing "the problem of 'speaking (as) woman' is precisely that of finding a possible continuity between that gestural expression or that speech of desire–which at present can only be identified in the form of symptoms and pathology–and a language, including a verbal language."[16] The impetus is that in speaking between the lines in a fashion less overt than Anne Lister, yet speaking nonetheless, Katharine and Edith developed their own lesbian poetics which allowed them to write of their desire in coded tones. To the knowing reader, it is not only their own psychical collaboration with Sappho in writing *Long Ago* that speaks volumes.

For the record, Katharine and Edith did not specifically state what they were, or what they were not. They did not once use the term "lesbian" to refer to their own relationship. The term was used to refer to Sappho, however, showing they had an appreciation for its meaning, while "lover" was an endearment bestowed not only on each other, but also on Edith's sister and their respective parents. Yet they loved each other, they needed each other, and they knew each other. The scholar who seeks will find what she needs.

Love nestles between their breasts.

Like most contemporary theorists, I want Katharine and Edith to be lovers in the most intimate sense. I want them to be lovers because I want to see myself in them, working together, loving together, expressing a desire both for and about each other and for the women in their lives. And so I write them as such. Yet my positioning of the couple as either same-sex lovers or otherwise is a construction affected by my own subjectivity and by my own cultural readings. This is not to deny their lesbian collaboration; indeed that is not, as far as I am concerned, up for dispute. What is open to question, however, is *their* interpretation, as well as ours, of what we now call a lesbian poetics and of what collaboration meant to them, of how it fed into their lives, both personal and professional. In doing so, we must dually ask how it is that we collaborate in the stories we tell. This cut-up has allowed me, the writer who reads, to play with this construction in accordance with the culture that informs reading/writing/reading–both then and now.

One of the great myths of collaboration is that it condenses multiple speaking positions into an unproblematic singular voice, that the act of creating is not charged with the tensions that must come in combining creative voices, that difference must always seep into sameness. As Virginia Blain has written, this is especially the case in lesbian collaboration which "runs the risk of being re-submerged into the wash of sameness which so commonly glazes over the woman-woman dyad."[17] The problem the Michael Field scholar faces is that Katharine and Edith did not want to be torn apart. Remember, "[w]e clasp each other with an awful weight of anxiety on our hearts, for they may strive to part us"[18] and "[t]his happy union of two in work and aspiration is sheltered and expressed by 'Michael Field.' Please regard him as the author."[19] What should the biographer/critic do? Should she honor their desire to keep together the "single individual"[20] created, the voice of Michael Field? Or should she take up the voyeuristic urge and prise the two bodies apart to explore what David Novarr terms "the architectonics of a life, in the relation of the parts to the whole"?[21] Should she seek to identify the structural elements that made up not simply the written life of "Michael Field" poet but also of the two *individuals* lurking behind the guise? It is a problem that faces any scholar who looks at collaboration. The natural instinct is to tear the collaborators apart; to break open the casing and pull out the bodies nestled within. For me, cutting up their work–literally taking scissors to the sentences they'd once carefully arranged–exposed the violence of the horror bound in separation. What do we scholars do when we deconstruct alternate stories, breaking them down into manageable bites? Why do we seek out collaboration as proof of desire, of difference, and then rip at their makers' seams with our theoretical teeth?

Throughout this cut-up the point of view changes. It begins with "we," with Michael Field speaking as "one" before splintering off into two individual voices and then concludes by begging the reader to consider the couple as one. Yet who is it that speaks–here and elsewhere? During the narrative the reader hears the voice of Edith, other times it is that of Katharine (or Sim or Michael, as she was also known). Between that comes the anonymous theoretical voice. By the end the final textual navigator does not know who speaks, who writes. Is it them, collectively, singularly? Or is it me? Who is ghosting the text? Who has taken over the pen, who guides it across the pages? Who is writing this now? Yes it is me, but it is also them. I am aware of the things they did not want to say. And so I collaborate, corroborate, to produce the final work. Our voices have merged. I return a poet possessing a Poet.[22]

Here I have wanted to show that my reading of Michael Field, and concurrently of Katharine and Edith as a biographical re-imagining, is a collaborative, partnering process. Together they help to make me, to re-vision me, while I, in turn, in accordance with my own desires and my own experiential cultural knowledge, help to make them. In this combined biographical discourse there is a past-present cross-over, a dipping and weaving of texts, metamorphosing into a collaborative biographical poesis to create a "we"–conscious or otherwise–on the page. As Kaplan and Rose write of their own collaborative practice: "'She' and 'I' metamorphose into 'we,' hypothetical, invisible, yet nonetheless articulate."[23] Bette London, writing about women's collaboration, puts it thus: "If these texts have interest, it is decidedly not as texts, in the sense of self-contained aesthetic units, and not as hidden keys to the author's biography. Their interest lies . . . in what they illuminate about the writing process."[24] Collaboration, she writes, is an unstable category representing a range of authored activities–assistance/ inspiration, mentoring/mutual influence, revision/editorial input.[25] It is writing, writing and writing again, it is a melting, a melding, a shaping, a becoming . . . Collaboration is cut-up is biography is writing.

CODA

The body is the place where our stories begin, where memories are re-membered, to be stitched into narratives that work to tell tales stretched across skin. How many times do we hear about "writing the body," "reading the body," "working the body"? Bodies are storehouses of memories, physical archives that render language silent: pain, love, joy, disappointment, suppression, repression, oppression. The body is a symphony of beginnings that begin again and again and again . . . the end of the beginning of the end.

Dead bodies provide fertile ground for telling. For in death silence speaks loudly. Death, that violence on life, allows us, the still-breathing, to grapple with living, to begin to untangle the knotty twists of our natal selves, our sexual selves, our mortal being. Telling stories about bodies helps the living to be, to understand through a continual state of making and unmaking. The other observed turned in.

Life unfolds from beginning to end, but for the teller of tales re-casting experience never progresses along linear lines. Then it is fragmented and incomplete, like shards of selves glittering across sands of too-distant shores, never to be pieced so wholly together again. Still we organize our-selves around these parts, strung into paper doll episodes, which in turn become our-narratives that find absences to plug up the hole.

Is it possible to enter that world? Can I slip between the sheets and move within your dreams? Can we walk together, talk together in time? When will you become more than a mark on my page? I want you to speak but it is only my voice that I hear.

Here, there, in this place and in that, in those fractures, I commence what has already become, and what is becoming, my place of knowing, my movingforwardsbackwards: my pilgrimage, my site of illumination, my making of a language-forming-speaking.

To silence. To absence. To imagination. Words threaded around an idea, an image. Pearls within ruins. Chaos and debris. A biographer laments. Dust to dust. Suspended in time. And then to a whisper. Pack up your world and imagine, they say. Come, link your arms with mine.

NOTES

1. Michel Foucault, *The History of Sexuality: An Introduction,* Trans. Robert Hurley, Peregrine Books, 1984.

2. Germaine Greer, *The Female Eunuch*, Paladin Books, London, 1971.

3. Luce Irigaray, *The Irigaray Reader*, Margaret Whitford (ed.), Blackwell Publishers, Oxford, 1991.

4. *Works and Days: From the Journal of Michael Field*, T.D. and D.C. Sturge Moore (eds.), John Murray, London, 1933.

5. As lifelong partners, united by an emotional, spiritual and intellectual synergy, Katharine and Edith found constraint in their femaleness, yet strength in their dual identities acted out through their collaboration, which they both articulated and denied, as part of a reciprocal daring double act. Through "Michael Field" they published a continuum of works–some 27 dramas, eight volumes of poetry and one masque–many of which, to varying degrees or another, focus on historical representations of women's same-sex desire.

6. The term "ghostly" is taken from Anna Gibbs who writes: "To compose a cut-up is both to ghost and to be ghosted by other writers," Gibbs in "Afterword," in *The Space Between: Australian Women Writing Fictocriticism*, Heather Kerr and Amanda Nettelbeck (eds.), University of Western Australia, Nedlands, 1998, p. 46.

7. Harold Nicolson, "The Practice of Biography," in *The Cornhill Magazine*, no. 996, Summer, 1953, p. 476.

8. Greer, op. cit., p. 20.

9. Ibid., p. 22.

10. See Whitney Chadwick and Isabelle de Courtivron "Introduction," *Significant Others: Creativity & Intimate Partnership*, Whitney Chadwick and Isabelle de Courtivron (eds.), Thames and Hudson, London, 1993, pp. 7-13.

11. Ibid., pp. 11-12.

12. Katharine and Edith frequently noted that once a work was complete, they could not tell who wrote what. This has been echoed by contemporary collaborators like Carey Kaplan and Ellen Cronan Rose, Sandra Gilbert and Susan Gubar, and Anne Brewster and Hazel Smith, who each collaborate on theoretical writings, as well as fiction writers Jacky Bratton and Jane Traies–the two voices behind the lesbian partnership/pseudonym represented by the pen name Jay Taverner.

13. Mary Sturgeon, *Michael Field*, G.G. Harrap, London, 1922, p. 75.

14. Field in Sturge Moore, op. cit., p. 16.

15. Ibid., p. 3.

16. Luce Irigaray in Whitfield op. cit., p. 138.

17. Virginia Blain, "'Michael Field, the two-headed nightingale': lesbian text as palimpsest," *Women's History Review*, vol. 5, no. 2, 1996, p. 241.

18. Field in Sturge Moore, op. cit., p. 50.

19. Ibid., p. 3.

20. Field in Sturge Moore, op. cit., p. 6.

21. David Novarr, *The Lines of Life: Theories of Biography, 1880-1970*, Purdue University Press, Indiana, 1986, p. ix.

22. Field in Sturge Moore, op. cit., p. 127.

23. Carey Kaplan and Ellen Cronan Rose, "Strange Bedfellows" in *Signs: Journal of Women in Culture and Society*, vol. 18, no. 3, Spring 1993, p. 549.

24. Bette London, *Writing Double: Women's Literary Relationships*, Cornell University Press, Ithaca and London, 1999, p. 29.

25. Ibid., p. 19.

Becoming
the "Professors of Lesbian Love"

Leila J. Rupp
Verta Taylor

University of California, Santa Barbara

SUMMARY. We tell here our all-too-unusual story of living and working together, reflecting on both the obstacles and the forces that made it possible for us to find each other, stay together, and develop a collabora-

---

Leila J. Rupp is Professor and Chair of Women's Studies at the University of California, Santa Barbara. A historian by training, her teaching and research focus on sexuality and women's movements. She is coauthor with Verta Taylor of *Drag Queens at the 801 Cabaret* (2003) and *Survival in the Doldrums: The American Women's Rights Movement, 1945 to the 1960s* (1987) and author of *A Desired Past: A Short History of Same-Sex Sexuality in America* (1999), *Worlds of Women: The Making of an International Women's Movement* (1997), and *Mobilizing Women for War: German and American Propaganda, 1939-1945* (1978).

Verta Taylor is Professor of Sociology at the University of California, Santa Barbara. She is coauthor with Leila J. Rupp of *Drag Queens at the 801 Cabaret* (University of Chicago Press) and *Survival in the Doldrums: The American Women's Rights Movement, 1945 to the 1960s* (Oxford University Press); co-editor with Laurel Richardson and Nancy Whittier of *Feminist Frontiers VI* (McGraw-Hill); and author of *Rock-a-by Baby: Feminism, Self-Help and Postpartum Depression* (Routledge). Her articles on the women's movement, the gay and lesbian movement, and social movement theory have appeared in journals such as *The American Sociological Review*, *Signs*, *Social Problems*, *Mobilization*, *Gender & Society*, *Qualitative Sociology*, *Journal of Women's History*, and *Journal of Homosexuality*.

[Haworth co-indexing entry note]: "Becoming the 'Professors of Lesbian Love.'" Rupp, Leila J., and Verta Taylor. Co-published simultaneously in *Journal of Lesbian Studies* (Harrington Park Press, an imprint of The Haworth Press, Inc.) Vol. 9, No. 4, 2005, pp. 25-39; and: *Lesbian Academic Couples* (ed: Michelle Gibson, and Deborah T. Meem) Harrington Park Press, an imprint of The Haworth Press, Inc., 2005, pp. 25-39. Single or multiple copies of this article are available for a fee from The Haworth Document Delivery Service [1-800-HAWORTH, 9:00 a.m. - 5:00 p.m. (EST). E-mail address: docdelivery@haworthpress.com].

Available online at http://www.haworthpress.com/web/JLS
doi:10.1300/J155v9n04_03

tive working relationship. Despite experiencing various forms of discrimination, we have been able over the years to contribute to the creation of a queer community through hiring lesbian colleagues, attracting lesbian and gay students, participating in the lesbian, gay, bisexual, and transgender movement, and advocating social justice for women and gay, lesbian, bisexual, and transgender people in our respective professional associations. This is the story of becoming the "professors of lesbian love," a title bestowed upon us by the drag queens we studied in our most recent joint project. *[Article copies available for a fee from The Haworth Document Delivery Service: 1-800-HAWORTH. E-mail address: <docdelivery@haworthpress.com> Website: <http://www.HaworthPress. com> © 2005 by The Haworth Press, Inc. All rights reserved.]*

KEYWORDS. Lesbian, academic couple, spousal hiring, domestic partner benefits, collaboration

The "professors of lesbian love": that's what the drag queens we studied for our most recent project took to calling us. It's a title we embrace, but one we probably could never have imagined would be bestowed on us the day we met. It was 1978, at the very beginning of the academic year, and the Office of Women's Studies at Ohio State University was sponsoring a Saturday morning panel on "The Legal Rights of Women in the United States." We met in the planning process for that panel, both of us new young faculty members. Leila was beginning her second year as an assistant professor of history and women's studies, and Verta, also in her second year on the faculty, was co-director of the Disaster Research Center and an assistant professor of sociology. We mark our years together from the day of that panel, even though we were both then in other relationships with women and took some time to ease out of them and into ours. So this is the story of how we became the professors of lesbian love.

In our quarter-century together, we have had the good fortune to work at the same school, to share intellectual interests, to collaborate on books and articles, and even to move to another university that hired both of us. We tell here our all-too-unusual story of living and working together, first at Ohio State University and now at the University of California, Santa Barbara, reflecting on both the obstacles and the forces that made it possible for us to find each other, stay together, develop a collaborative working relationship, and thrive because we continue to enjoy each other's company. Over the years at Ohio State, we were able to contribute to the creation of a queer community through hiring lesbian colleagues, attracting lesbian and gay students, participating in the lesbian, gay, bisexual, and transgender movement both on and off campus, and advocating social justice for women and gay, lesbian, bisexual, and transgender people in our respective professional associations. In that way, we hope we have "paid forward" some of the debts we acquired through the years.

BEGINNINGS

When we met, it was still possible for the Office of Women's Studies at Ohio State to sponsor an annual reception for all women faculty in a university of over fifty thousand students, and the room wasn't even overflowing. So our story begins with getting to the university in the first place. Verta grew up in Jonesboro, Arkansas, not far from Memphis, and she was the first in her family to attend college. Her father, who had only an eighth-grade education, was adamantly opposed to her leaving, so she ended up at Indiana State University, a long day's drive from home. He had suffered a heart attack in his thirties and died after her first year in college, but her mother, who went to work as a secretary, somehow managed to scrape together the money for Verta to finish. As a student activist with a passion for the study of social movements, she was recruited as a graduate student to Ohio State by the late Clyde Franklin, a young African American faculty member who had grown up in Birdsong, an all-Black town near Jonesboro. A new young assistant professor, he had the task of recruiting minority students. Between her name (Verta, her grandmother's name, is more typically African American) and her campus activism around civil rights issues, Clyde was sure she was Black. Only after offering her a fellowship did he ask and find out that she isn't. The university substituted another fellowship for which she qualified, and when they became colleagues, they always laughed about the story. He also turned out to be gay and an important influence on her career as a graduate student and later as a faculty member.

Verta went to work as a graduate student at the Disaster Research Center, a well-funded center focusing on the sociological impact of natural and man-made disasters. She moved quickly up the ranks to field director and then co-director with her advisor, who was deeply involved in her career as a teacher and mentor. Without her knowledge, he arranged for her to move into a faculty position and remain as co-director when she completed her dissertation, going so far as to refuse to write letters of recommendation for her to other schools because he did not want her to leave. Hiring one's own graduate student was, of course, as unusual at Ohio State as at other universities. After all of this was arranged, what she had thought of as a close but professional relationship turned out to be something else altogether when he announced that he was in love with her, despite the fact that he knew that she lived with a woman. This was all in the days before universities had developed policies against sexual harassment. Eventually the situation became intolerable, so she resigned her co-directorship, giving up all of the benefits of the position. When she told the chair of the Department of Sociology the reason she was resigning, he made sure that she would still have a tenure-track appointment in the department.

Leila had a much more privileged educational background, having grown up in a white, professional family in New Jersey. She attended Bryn Mawr College, where the Quaker influence connected her to her mother's heritage and where the emphasis on strong women appealed to her as-yet-unnamed feminist sensibilities. During the heady summer of 1969, in summer school in Boston, she read Simone de Beauvoir and encountered what was then called "female liberation." She took a class with Herbert Aptheker on Black history and sat in on Kate Millett's class on women's studies. She found Bryn Mawr wonderfully nurturing, so when she began to apply to graduate schools and found little support in the world outside for her interest in German women's history, it came as something of a shock. After a trying year at the University of North Carolina, she returned to Bryn Mawr to earn her PhD. The unconventional decision to earn a graduate degree at a women's college, combined with the fact that she wrote a dissertation in comparative women's history that did not place her squarely in a traditional historical field, limited her options in a difficult job market. So Leila felt incredibly fortunate when she was hired as the first faculty member in women's studies at Ohio State in a job advertised as either European or American women's history.

These beginnings are significant because both of us, in different ways, came into our tenuring departments through the back door. Although the history department participated in the search, Leila's faculty position had been initiated by women's studies, and it is not clear that most members of the history faculty at that time would have chosen to hire a women's historian. The story that went around about the creation of the job attributed it to the traditional football rivalry with the University of Michigan: Michigan had just started a women's studies program, so Ohio State threw more money into its unit. This may be true, but the very presence of an Office of Women's Studies, albeit without faculty or courses, had come about through feminist protests on campus.

AGAINST THE ODDS

So when we met that Saturday, we both knew that we were in some ways there against the odds. And now we think, for a whole raft of other reasons, that we were incredibly fortunate to survive academically through the turbulent years that followed. Verta, the night before the panel, had celebrated her one-year anniversary with a woman lover. Leila was technically married to a man but involved in a long-distance relationship with a woman. She never did find out what faculty members in history, some of whom at least knew that she was married, thought about the fact that suddenly there seemed to be no husband.

Furthermore, Verta had to create a whole new research agenda and teaching profile when she left disaster research. After she earned tenure, she moved into women's studies, which had begun to add faculty, develop courses, and become a regular academic unit. And then we both left women's studies as the result of one of those political blowups that used to occur with some regularity in such units. We attribute the upheaval in women's studies at least partly to resentment of our relationship. At the time, we said that the problem was that we were a happy lesbian couple, and some people didn't like the lesbian, some didn't like the couple, and some didn't like the happy. The whole experience was extremely traumatic. Leila, who had begun her academic career in women's studies, had to develop a whole new set of courses as a full-time historian. For Verta, it meant retooling once again. But we survived that, too, both professionally and as a couple, and the transition provided us an opportunity to bring feminism and gay/lesbian studies more squarely into our respective departments.

We are well aware of our privilege in the world of lesbian academic couples. We both already had positions at the same university when we met, so we did not have to try to be hired as a couple the first time around. We did not have to try to maintain a long distance relationship. This is not to say, however, that we encountered no obstacles.

We both experienced some of the forms of discrimination that Verta wrote about with her graduate student, Nicole Raeburn, now an assistant professor and chair of the Department of Sociology at the University of San Francisco, based on a survey of gay, lesbian, and bisexual sociologists (Taylor and Raeburn 1995). They found that faculty members whose research, publishing, and teaching focused on queer topics, who mentored lesbian, gay, and bisexual students and colleagues, and who advocated equality on the basis of sexual identity in the university and profession were more likely to encounter discrimination than those who were out but not active in these ways. They identified five kinds of negative consequences: discrimination in hiring, bias in tenure and promotion, exclusion from social and professional networks, devaluation of scholarly work on queer topics, and harassment and intimidation. To lesser and greater extents, we experienced all of these at some point in time.

DISCRIMINATION IN HIRING

When we were hired at Ohio State, neither of us was totally out and neither of us was working on lesbian or gay research topics. But over the years, we occasionally applied for other positions, primarily because Verta's department, after she left women's studies, was for many years quite hostile to qualitative and feminist research. Going on the job market, we experienced what is all too familiar to most lesbian couples. A southern university contacted Verta about applying for an endowed chair, and the search committee recommended that she be brought in for an interview. But then, as a feminist colleague there told Verta, at a faculty meeting she was dropped from the list because her research on lesbians and drag queens would be too controversial for the donor of the chair.

Until we were hired at the University of California, no institution made much effort to hire us as a couple. Once Verta was interviewed for the position of director of women's studies at a major university, and at the first dinner with the search committee, a senior woman historian made it clear that Leila would never be hired. She also argued, Verta later learned, that it would not be a good idea to have an open lesbian as head of women's studies.

In the history department, Leila saw several times the workings that are mostly hidden from us as lesbian or gay academics. A scholar working on the history of same-sex sexuality would be eliminated from the pool of potential candidates because she or he was not deemed to fit the job description of social history or political history. A close colleague told Leila that one of their male colleagues described a lesbian candidate working on a mainstream topic, who was brought in for an interview, as "that radical lesbian." Our students worried about having "lavender vitae," and even the most activist students sometimes cleaned them up in hopes it would help them on the job market.

BIAS IN TENURE AND PROMOTION

We were both tenured the same year, in 1982. One of the closeted gay men in Leila's department told her that the college-level committee had inquired whether she taught from "a lesbian perspective" because she had published a piece about lesbian history. In Verta's tenure interview with her department, a male colleague asked her whether she was a sociologist or "in women's studies," and one of her outside reviewers referred to one of her pieces about the women's movement as "passionate" and "polemical." Verta's department also asked her why she had spent her time editing *Feminist Frontiers* (now in a sixth edition), the first women's studies text to incorporate a great deal of material on lesbians (Richardson and Taylor 1983). Yet we both flew through the tenure process without other incident and even received a congratulatory telephone call from the then-provost, Ann Reynolds, who knew of our relationship and has remained a good friend over the years.

Promotion to full professor turned out to be more difficult for Verta. Despite her extensive record of publication, some of her colleagues discounted the qualitative and feminist work that she did, especially her research on lesbian topics. Ironically, Leila was promoted on the basis of a book they coauthored, for which Verta barely received a raise. Verta had to publish many more articles and another book–having nothing to do with lesbians–before she was promoted.

EXCLUSION FROM SOCIAL NETWORKS

We both felt excluded from social networks in our departments for many years, although that changed over time. One senior member of Verta's department was rumored to have kept a list of department members who were not to be invited to social events at his house, complete with reason, such as "divorced." We could only imagine what might be listed next to Verta's name! Until a string of feminist women chaired the sociology department, we were never invited as a couple to departmental functions. We made our social worlds outside our departments, at first in women's studies and later with friends outside the university.

In 1999, Leila became the first woman chair of the history department, and Verta, with new feminist leadership in place in her department, took on a major role, first as chair of the search committee and then as director of undergraduate studies. These new positions were both recognition of our growing centrality to our departments and opportunities to bring about change from within. We were instrumental in hiring younger and more congenial colleagues, including our first lesbian colleagues, Birgitte Søland in history and Nella Van Dyke in sociology. No longer were we the only lesbians at departmental social events, which we were now more likely to attend and even sometimes to organize.

DEVALUATION OF SCHOLARLY WORK

Both of us know that over the years some of our colleagues looked askance at our work on lesbian and gay topics. No senior members of Verta's department expressed any interest in her work in those areas, and one close feminist colleague even advised her not to discuss her research in department colloquia. Perhaps to protect her when she came up for promotion to professor, the sociology department's official report on her research made no mention of Verta's work on gay and lesbian movements. The omission was glaring since her article on lesbian feminist communities (Taylor and Whittier 1992) is her most frequently cited and reprinted piece. Similarly, when Leila proposed writing a module on the gay and lesbian movement for *Retrieving the American Past,* the highly successful departmentally produced electronic reader, a senior colleague said that the topic was "silly," but if she wanted to do it, she should go ahead. One generally supportive senior feminist colleague in another department advised Leila not to reprint her article about women's relationships, "Imagine My Surprise" (Rupp 1980), because she would one day be embarrassed by it. As it turns out, it is one of her most cited and reprinted articles.

HARASSMENT AND INTIMIDATION

We both have experienced various forms of harassment and intimidation. One of Verta's male colleagues once commented in the hall, in response to the large number of lesbian students who came to study with her at Ohio State, that women students came into the department with long hair and boyfriends and then cut their hair and got girlfriends. When Leila introduced a course on the history of same-sex sexuality in the western world, she encountered resistance from graduate school committee members who wondered how she could teach such a course with both undergraduate and graduate students, even though all the courses at that level throughout the university targeted both audiences. Students sometimes made homophobic comments on their course evaluations. One of Verta's students in her introductory sociology course of seven hundred students once wrote, "I don't think the university should allow dykes to teach this course." Leila once had to endure a hostile white man sitting through her class on the history of same-sexuality with a sneer on his face and an objection to the reading at every turn. And we both have had flyers on our office doors defaced with comments about "dykes."

More seriously, when Verta was on a site visit for a National Institute of Mental Health project on community disaster planning in rural Arkansas, she was raped at gunpoint at an isolated motel by a man who called her a "dyke." At that time, she had very short hair, did not shave her legs, and was wearing overalls, evidently all clear signals about her sexuality. She noticed a man staring at her at the pool, and later when she went to get ice, he followed her and stuck a gun in her back as she opened the door to her room. Alone in a strange place, she was afraid to call the police and never reported the rape. It was the kind of trauma that has serious consequences, not just personally but professionally as well. Verta was not yet tenured and lost a lot of time that summer as she worked through the depression that followed, and she never again accepted an invitation to participate in such a site visit.

We don't mean to dwell on the negative experiences, but it is important to recognize the costs as well as the benefits of commitment to lesbian and gay scholarship and activism and living openly as a lesbian couple. We know at a personal level, as Verta points out in her work with Nicole Raeburn (Taylor and Raeburn 1995), that identity politics can be both constraining and enabling. The forms of discrimination we describe here have ruined the academic careers and personal lives of other scholars. In the end, we have benefited far more than we have suffered from our decisions to teach and research queer topics, but we believe that, in part, it is the strength of our relationship that allowed us to thrive and to live creative lives. We were honored when the *Chronicle of Higher Education* in 2004–twenty-six years after we first met–chose to feature us as one of three academic couples for a Valentine's Day feature called "Academic Allure."

BUILDING COMMUNITY

There was something else that made it possible for us to survive and even flourish at Ohio State. Above all, it was a network of gay/lesbian faculty, staff, and students. At first that network was centered in women's studies. One of our gay men friends used to joke that gay men at the university had to meet in gossiped-about bathrooms, while we found each other at women's studies. It was true that it was, in those days, a magnet for lesbian scholars who often found little support in their home departments. Leila would probably not have been hired without women's studies, and women's studies provided a home for Verta when she felt she had to leave the Disaster Research Center.

There were also individuals who played a critical role in forging connections among gay, lesbian, and bisexual members of the university and larger community. Most important was Rhonda Rivera, a law professor and activist who paved the way for others in the university. Rhonda was on that panel where we met, and she spoke out continually in support of gay and lesbian faculty, staff, and students. Verta used to joke that the way one came out on campus and found out if someone else was what we referred to in those days as a "person like us" was to ask, "Do you know Rhonda Rivera?" It was Rhonda who sparked the formation of a campus group, the Association of Gay, Lesbian, and Bisexual Faculty and Staff, where we struggled and failed to win recognition of and benefits for domestic partners. It was Rhonda who got us involved in Stonewall Union, the gay and lesbian community group that she helped found.

We, in turn, were able to contribute to the creation of a lesbian, gay, bisexual, and transgender community. Over time, we began to teach gay and lesbian courses and to advise students working on queer topics. Verta, in fact, has been dubbed the "lesbian den mother of sociology" for having mentored so many lesbian students and junior colleagues (Taylor 2003). Often our lesbian graduate students provided us as much support as we gave to them. In two cases, graduate students working with each of us formed lasting relationships, creating what feels like an enduring lesbian family. Verta's student and coauthor, Nancy Whittier, now at Smith College, and Leila's student Kate Weigand, who works at the Sophia Smith Collection, live in Northampton with their three children. Elizabeth Kaminski and Stephanie Gilmore, our research assistants when we were working on the drag queen book, fell in love and moved together to West Hartford, where Betsy is an assistant professor of sociology at Central Connecticut College and Stephanie is finishing her dissertation. We are very proud of their relationships as well as their wonderful scholarly accomplishments.

We both became active in our respective professional caucuses for lesbian, gay, bisexual, and transgender issues as well. Verta chaired the Committee on the Status of Gay, Lesbian, Bisexual, and Transgender Sociologists, and Leila has served on the board of the Committee on Lesbian and Gay History. All of these different networks connected us to other lesbian scholars and activists and provided support for our work on campus, in the Columbus community, and in the profession.

WORKING TOGETHER

We have saved the best for last: our work together. Even before we lived together, we began to collaborate on a study of the U.S. women's movement in the 1950s. Leila had begun the research, and when she met Verta and learned of her expertise and experience in large-scale interviewing projects at the Disaster Research Center, she asked if she would be interested in working together. That led to our first joint book, *Survival in the Doldrums*, supported by a large grant from the National Endowment for the Humanities (Rupp and Taylor 1987). From the beginning, we were intellectually compatible. Leila's training as a historian fit perfectly with Verta's preference for qualitative methods that result in the development of situated knowledge located in a particular time and space. Yet we had and continue to have our different strengths. Verta is the theorist and interviewer, Leila the crafter of narrative and archival researcher. Together we conceptualize projects, discuss interpretations, revise, and even sometimes sit and write at the computer, at the kitchen table, or (our favorite) at the beach.

We continue to work both separately and together, and we take special pride in the way our collaborative work moves beyond what either of us could produce alone. It is truly interdisciplinary, not just the scotch-taping together of sociology and history. *Survival in the Doldrums*, for example, details the history of a women's movement during a time no one thought there was one. But we moved beyond that particular history to understand how movements survive in inhospitable climates and what impact that survival has on the recruitment possibilities,

strategies, and goals of such movements. Verta went on to publish a theoretical article about such "abeyance phases" in the premier sociology
journal (Taylor 1989), and the concept of abeyance has become a staple
of social movement theory.

We then wrote together about lesbian feminist communities, combining ethnographic and participatory research in Columbus and at national events with analysis of written sources and interviews (Taylor
and Rupp 1993). Building on Verta's work with Nancy Whittier (Taylor
and Whittier 1992), we argued that, far from leading to the demise of
feminism, the culture of lesbian feminist communities both served as a
base of mobilization for women involved in a wide range of social
movements and provided continuity from earlier stages of the women's
movement.

In both of these projects, our identity as lesbians and feminists played
a crucial role. In writing about feminists in the 1950s, we saw that
women's relationships played a critical role in holding the movement
together, as well as in limiting recruitment to a homogeneous group of
women. In the papers of individuals and organizations, we found evidence of women who lived together in marriage-like relationships and
formed communities with similar couples. We grappled with the question of whether or not some of these women were lesbians and also with
whether or not it mattered. Our identities as lesbians probably made us
more aware of women's connections to other women, but they also may
have made us too cautious in our inquiries. We hesitated to raise the issue directly because we feared that bringing up lesbianism with women
who ranged in age from their mid-60s to their early 80s would impose
contemporary conceptions and violate the atmosphere of the interaction. In contrast, the second project simply would have been impossible
without being involved over a long period of time in the lesbian feminist
community (Taylor and Rupp 1996, Rupp and Taylor 2002).

We have written many other articles and chapters together on
women's movements and gay and lesbian movements and communities, but we want to end our story with our most recent book, *Drag
Queens at the 801 Cabaret* (Rupp and Taylor 2003). Sometimes we ask
ourselves, how did we as lesbian scholars end up studying a bunch of
men in dresses? It was, in fact, the perfect project in so many ways because it has to do with gender, sexuality, and the performance of protest.
The troupe of drag queens we studied is in Key West, Florida, which
had become our escape beginning when we were assistant professors
from the cold and conservatism of Ohio to a gay world. We made use of
Verta's knowledge of social movement theory and experience with in-

terviewing, ethnographic, and participatory research and Leila's penchant for writing for a popular audience. For over three years, we interviewed drag queens (and some of their mothers and boyfriends), attended and taped the shows, went to drag queen meetings and parties, read the local media, and ran focus groups with audience members to find out why people (men, women, straight, gay, lesbian, bisexual, transgendered, transsexual, tourists, locals) come to the shows and what they think and feel. We found out that what the drag queens intend–to make their audiences think in a more complex way about gender and sexuality–was just what happened. We came to think that drag shows have political consequences, that they embody protest and build a complex collective identity across genders and sexualities. We use this study to enter into the debate among social movement scholars about what makes cultural forms political at the same time that we offer an accessible and sexy narrative that led one reviewer to describe the book as "an entertaining amalgam of scholarship and sassiness."[1]

IMAGINE OUR SURPRISE

After twenty-five years at Ohio State, we had the amazing good fortune to be hired as a couple at the University of California, Santa Barbara. That also had to do with networks of support, for, as everyone knows, hiring a lesbian academic couple doesn't happen without a lot of work on the part of many savvy people. In this case, the Women's Studies Program, along with Verta's longtime friend and lesbian colleague Beth Schneider, with a lot of help from feminist and gender scholar Sarah Fenstermaker and social movements scholar Dick Flacks, somehow produced the miracle of two jobs. In some ways, the move seems like the culmination of our life and work together. After struggling for so many years at Ohio State for health benefits for domestic partners, something the state legislature adamantly opposed, we entered a system that provides full benefits for domestic partners in a state that grants almost the same legal rights to domestic partners as to married couples.[2]

We continue to work at the University of California to make queer space. Leila serves as co-chair of Eucalyptus, the campus-wide gay, lesbian, bisexual, and transgender organization, and she took responsibility for the final stages of a proposal for a new minor in queer studies, which many on campus had worked long and hard to make a reality. Recently, we brought three of the drag queens we studied from Key West to Santa Barbara, where they performed in Verta's seven hundred stu-

dent introductory sociology class, participated in a panel discussion
with drag kings, and put on a Friday night show at the Multicultural
Center. The extensive and enthusiastic publicity in the student and local
alternative paper made clear that the drag queens' message about the
fluidity of gender and sexuality got across.

So, against all the odds, and much to our surprise, we found each other,
fashioned a creative personal and intellectual life together, flourished,
and have every intention of living happily ever after. We are always
mindful of the women's movement activism that made it possible for us
to go to graduate school and become faculty members in the first place, as
well as the gay/lesbian activism that made it possible for us to come out
and write about gay and lesbian topics and still get published and promoted and hired as a lesbian couple. We have been part of both struggles,
our participation was central to our success, and we have tried to pass on
to our students a commitment to social justice. We wrote about the drag
queens "performing protest," and we hope that we, too, as professors of
lesbian love, will continue to perform protest and make it possible for
other lesbians and gay men and bisexual and transgendered people further to transform the face of the university and the larger society.

NOTES

1. Review by Richard Labonte, on Gaywired.com, June 2003.
2. Editors' note: The Ohio State University, along with three other state-supported
universities in Ohio, granted domestic partner benefits to its employees in 2004.

REFERENCES

Richardson, Laurel and Verta Taylor, eds. 1983. *Feminist Frontiers: Rethinking Sex,
Gender, and Society.* Reading: Addison-Wesley.
Rupp, Leila J. 1980. "Imagine My Surprise: Women's Relationships in Historical Per-
spective." *Frontiers* 5: 61-70.
Rupp, Leila J. and Verta Taylor. 1987. *Survival in the Doldrums: The American
Women's Movement, 1945 to the 1960s.* New York: Oxford University Press.
_____. 2002. "Pauli Murray: The Unasked Question." *Journal of Women's History*
14: 79-83.
_____. 2003. *Drag Queens at the 801 Cabaret.* Chicago: University of Chicago Press.
Taylor, Verta. 1989. "Social Movement Continuity: The Women's Movement in
Abeyance." *American Sociological Review* 54: 761-75.
_____. 2003. "My Life in Social Movements: From 1960s Activist to Lesbian Den
Mother." In *Our Studies, Ourselves: Sociologists' Lives and Work*, edited by Barry
Glassner and Rosanna Hertz, pp. 263-78. New York: Oxford University Press.

Taylor, Verta and Nicole C. Raeburn. 1995. "Identity Politics as High-Risk Activism: Career Consequences for Lesbian, and Bisexual Sociologists." *Social Problems* 42: 252-73.

Taylor, Verta and Leila J. Rupp. 1993. "Women's Culture and Lesbian Feminist Activism: A Reconsideration of Cultural Feminism." *Signs: Journal of Women in Culture and Society* 19: 32-61.

_____. 1996. "Lesbian Existence and the Women's Movement: Researching the 'Lavender Herring'." In *Feminism and Social Change: Bridging Theory and Practice,* edited by Heidi Gottfriend, pp. 143-59. Champaign-Urbana: University of Illinois Press.

Taylor, Verta and Nancy Whittier. 1992. "Collective Identity in Social Movement Communities: Lesbian Feminist Mobilization." Pp. 104-129 in *Frontiers in Social Movement Theory,* eds. Aldon Morris and Carol Mueller. New Haven: Yale University Press.

We're Both Tenured Professors . . . but Where Is Home?

Mary Frances Stuck

SUNY Oswego

Mary Ware

SUNY Cortland

SUMMARY. Mills' sociological imagination is used to look at relevant issues in the life of a lesbian academic couple in a distance relationship. Analysis includes concerns which are common to both lesbian and heterosexual couples in distance situations such as finding jobs, tenure, productivity, mentoring, managing two households, communication,

Mary Frances Stuck is Professor of Sociology and Assistant Dean of Arts & Sciences at SUNY Oswego (NY) where she has taught since 1985. She holds a PhD from Syracuse University in sociology. Her major teaching/research interests include equity issues: gender, affectional orientation, race/ethnicity. She and Mary Ware have been together since 1978 and have maintained a "family home" in Homer, NY, since 1980.

Mary Ware is Professor in the Department of Foundations and Social Advocacy at SUNY Cortland (NY) where she has taught since 1969. She holds a PhD from Syracuse University in instructional design, development and evaluation. Her major research interests include gender issues in education and women and computing. She and Mary Stuck have been together since 1978 and have maintained a "family home" in Homer, NY, since 1980.

The authors would like to thank Karen Shockey, Penfield Library, SUNY Oswego, for her diligence in finding the few resources on lesbian academic couples.

[Haworth co-indexing entry note]: "We're Both Tenured Professors . . . but Where Is Home?" Stuck, Mary Frances, and Mary Ware. Co-published simultaneously in *Journal of Lesbian Studies* (Harrington Park Press, an imprint of The Haworth Press, Inc.) Vol. 9, No. 4, 2005, pp. 41-56; and: *Lesbian Academic Couples* (ed: Michelle Gibson, and Deborah T. Meem) Harrington Park Press, an imprint of The Haworth Press, Inc., 2005, pp. 41-56. Single or multiple copies of this article are available for a fee from The Haworth Document Delivery Service [1-800-HAWORTH, 9:00 a.m. - 5:00 p.m. (EST). E-mail address: docdelivery@haworthpress.com].

community, and those items unique to lesbian couples–coming out to students, finding and maintaining a lesbian community, effects of hiring practices in academe. Based on the analysis, recommendations are presented. *[Article copies available for a fee from The Haworth Document Delivery Service: 1-800-HAWORTH. E-mail address: <docdelivery@haworthpress.com> Website: <http://www.HaworthPress.com>* © *2005 by The Haworth Press, Inc. All rights reserved.]*

KEYWORDS. Long-distance relationships, lesbian, home, academic couple

INTRODUCTION

In the spirit of C. Wright Mills' sociological imagination, which asks us to view the world through a lens that focuses on the intersection of history, biography and cultures (Mills, 1959), we plan to examine our careers as lesbian academics (with 17 and 32 years of experience) and as a lesbian couple (for 25 of those years). The methodology we utilize is well established historiography, the use of historical data to construct meaningful explanations of phenomena (Denzin, 1978), and oral traditions/histories (our own) to examine aspects of our lives as a lesbian academic couple who work at different institutions, far enough from each other that separate living units (at least during the academic year) must be maintained. Our lives will be used to examine issues relevant to academic couples in general, e.g., finding jobs in proximity to each other; the pressures for *two* to gain tenure; managing household(s); competition; mentoring. We will also examine issues particular to lesbian academics, e.g., "informal and unofficial rejection in academe" (Miller and Skeen in Ferber and Loeb: 1997: 119), "coming out"; finding and keeping a job; how one is viewed by students, fellow faculty and administrators; acknowledgment of one's partner.

Although literature suggests that lesbians may be "overrepresented in academia and among gay couples" (Miller & Skeen in Ferber & Loeb, 1997: 107), nearly all of the literature dealing with academic couples that we located references data from academic couples who are heterosexual. We will be looking for similarities and differences in the lives of these subjects and our own lived experiences, and the limited data from lesbian (or gay) academic couples.

ORAL HISTORY DATA

"... [F]irst person accounts such as oral histories and biographies are necessary if a researcher is to understand the subjectivity of a social group that has been 'muted, excised from history [and] invisible in the official records of their culture'" (Long, 1987:5 in Berg, 2001: 221). Our oral histories, which follow, are the foundation, the particulars upon which thematic theoretical analyses and comparisons will be made.

Ware is a professor of Foundations and Social Advocacy, where her colleagues know that she is a lesbian, in a school of education at State University of New York, College at Cortland, a small town in central New York State. She "came out" to herself just two years before taking a job as an instructor at this same college, 32 years ago. She has proceeded through the ranks of instructor, assistant professor, associate professor and professor, attaining that rank before she turned 40. (She has also been Director of Summer Sessions, Chair of the Education Department, Associate Dean of Professional Studies, and Graduate Dean.) She worked hard, tried to keep below the radar and was constantly worried (until she was tenured) that her affectional orientation might somehow keep her from obtaining continuing appointment–reflective of the history of the times. Once that hurdle was over, she became a little less paranoid; however, she has never been (until recent years) an "out" lesbian academic. In fact, when she authored a chapter in *Lesbians in Academia* (Mintz and Rothblum, 1997), she was not willing to have it published under her name. She was also a member of the school board in her *very small* hometown and was worried that coming out would undermine her effectiveness there. She still has concerns about coming out to students en masse. She does reveal herself to them when it seems appropriate (e.g., a student struggling with her identity). She brings her partner to any social events that allow a partner/spouse/guest and assumes that "most people know" (Anonymous in Mintz and Rothblum: 199-202).

Stuck is a professor of sociology who teaches in the Honors Program and who is also Assistant Dean of Arts and Sciences at SUNY Oswego, 82 miles from SUNY Cortland. She "came out" in the early 1970s, but not professionally, spent her early years in academe in student personnel administration, and returned to higher education to work on her PhD in the 1980s. She moved to Cortland, lived with her partner (Ware) and worked as an adjunct in as many as three institutions at once while finishing her degree. In 1985 she finally secured a tenure track position.

While Ware was secure in her tenured position, the issue of Stuck being an adjunct did not seem to pose any real problems; this was just part of the process of gaining the PhD, then a real job. Once the position was secured (1985), until tenure was granted, the problems were more about learning what political games had to be played in order to get tenure (Stuck served in two departments with official appointment in one–the system has no provision for dual appointment). Of course, this process then created relationship challenges as the senior, tenured partner (Ware) told the untenured one (Stuck) about the games and how to play them (see mentoring, later).

After the job search, and several abortive attempts to obtain employment at each other's institution, Stuck and Ware began to realize that they were likely to be a "commuting dual career academic couple" with two places of residence until one of them retired. Dr. Stuck is more "out" in her career than Ware–having given many rousing talks to GLBT groups and guest lectures in classes at SUNY Oswego, advising many students and some faculty on life as a lesbian. Sociology is perhaps a more "liberal" discipline in which to be "who you are"; however, Stuck is more active in "causes" and probably would have been "out" no matter what her discipline. After living in a two-room apartment over a garage for eight years, Dr. Stuck purchased a condominium in Oswego and lives there during the week.

Our "family home" is in Homer, New York, within three miles of SUNY Cortland. It was purchased by Ware and Stuck together in 1983, before Stuck had finished her PhD or found any permanent employment. Homer is where Ware and Stuck call "home" though given the fact that we live apart, home may more accurately in some senses be "where the heart is."

These various dimensions of our lives certainly create classic examples of Peter Berger's (1963) multiple levels of reality, for example, the reality of a physical building called home paired with the reality of not living in the same place; being someone (a lesbian) but having to hide it to be a school board member; the allowances for difference in academic disciplines and across time.

SINGLE RESIDENCE VS. DUAL RESIDENCE: STRESSORS

Literature has documented the difficulty of academic couples (mostly heterosexual) in "finding two positions that will permit both partners to live in the same geographic region, to address their professional goals and to meet the day to day needs of running a household" (Wolf-Wendell, Twombly and Rice, 2000:1). It is also well documented that many couples cannot find this living situation (same geographic location) and thus commute between geographically distant institutions (Bruce, 1990; Sorcinelli and Near, 1989; Wolf-Wendell, Twombly and Rice, 2000). Quality of life issues permeate all couplehoods. Comparison of dual residence vs. single residence couples may shatter some taken-for-granted assumptions, and may confirm others, as will be explored below: stressors related to workload responsibilities, meaning of "home," expenses, communication.

A study by Bunker, Zubek, Vanderslice and Rice (1992) used satisfaction (specifically work life satisfaction) and stress as indicators of quality of life. These two indicators are useful in analyzing our lives as case studies, with stress related to two different residences being examined first.

The most obvious problem with a distance relationship is that if one location is identified as "home," both partners cannot be there all the time. A product of this is stress related to the "workload of maintaining two households and the restructured division of labor" (Bunker & Vanderslice, 1982 in Bunker, Zubek, Vanderslice, and Rice, 1992: 401). Deliveries to the house (e.g., UPS) and scheduling of repair or home improvement work also must be coordinated. Many workers come only (unless one pays time and a half) on weekdays. If one individual is 82 miles away and the other is "at work" locally, scheduling such things as repair visits can be a nightmare. Obviously this issue is a problem for any couple, but academics usually have times when they can be home during the day, even on a day they teach or do research. For us, however, during the week Stuck is entirely away (unavailable for such things as repair calls even if she had time between classes or responsibilities), leaving it to Ware to schedule such calls and also to be there when repairpersons come. Car repair issues add additional problems. In a two car couple living in the same location, an issue like a car repair is not a problem, as individuals can share a ride—not so when living in two locations. These dynamics of trying to maintain two residences have created stressors for both members of this couple. However, over time these new roles (e.g., Ware becoming more responsible for the Homer residence) align with the findings of Bunker et al. (1992:404): "commuters did not report . . . a more stressful lifestyle than did single-residence dual-career couples." This lack of a more stressful life is probably a result of "some restructuring in the commuting two-residence couple that simplifies life or perceptions of it" (1992:405). Likewise, our redefined domestic roles reflect Miller and

Skeen's observation that "[e]galitarian relationship norms seem to be even more prevalent among gay and lesbian couples" than among any other kind of couple (p. 110 in Ferber and Loeb, 1997; Schneider, 1986; Larson, 1992).

If one values eating meals together, enjoying a fireplace, talking over the day's events, and falling to sleep together, even perhaps sharing the joy of having a family pet, the biggest cost in a distance relationship is exactly that–not sharing the same physical *home* during the week. Ware is in Homer all week; however she would quickly add that it does not seem like *home* during the week. Neither of us spends the time to prepare interesting meals, light the fire in the fireplace (only the Homer house has one), or do much other than open the mail, watch a bit of TV, continue working on academic pursuits, and fall asleep on nights apart. We *do* (and have, ever since we got together) talk by phone every night. This has its good and bad points that we will discuss later. Our family pet, a Lhasa Apso named Peanut, died in 1994 and we have not obtained another, both because we travel a lot and because it would have to live with only one of us during the week.

Many authors have explicated the importance of "home" for individuals. Others have studied the effect of homelessness on individuals. Obviously, the two of us have places to live–but since only one of them is "our home" Stuck does experience some loss when she is not there. Rabuzzi points out "the ability of the symbol *home* to hold an individual together" (Rabuzzi, 1982: 64). She continues, "Often home serves as a Jungian mandala, a symbol of integrated selfhood or wholeness." For the person who is "away from home" commuting, there is a periodic loss of this integration. We experience the loss of integration weekly in the Sunday night ritual in which Stuck prepares to go back to her workplace–taking "pieces" of "home" with her: meals to be reheated (left over from Sunday dinner), clothes from the closet, items needed for the week away.

The second obvious problem with the two household way of living is cost: we have two mortgages, two sets of utility bills, multiple sets of taxes, cell phone bills, landline and Internet bills, excessive gas costs and costs of putting extra miles on two cars. Even grocery shopping has to be multiplied–with the added cost of buying smaller packages of items for the condo, which is lived in only 4 out of 7 days per week. (The condo is also vacant in January, June, July and August, but costs continue whether anyone is there or not.)

COMMUNICATION

The issues of distance and time lead to another potential problem that plagues all commuting couples and that is communication. Does one talk by phone every day or night? How does the business of a "joint couple" get carried out? From the mundane issues of making physician and dentist appointments to the more complex issues of planning travel, home repair and working on relationships, it is essential to talk often. E-mail, since it has become ubiquitous, has made a remarkable difference in our communication. A Telocity survey documents this change in communication.

> When it comes to long-distance relationships, connecting is often a point-and-click away . . . 86% of couples in long-distance relationships responding to an online questionnaire use the Internet to keep in touch . . .

Through the online search, Telocity found that over 50% of couples in long-distance relationships see each other twice a month or less, but spend up to 10 hours a week online chatting and e-mailing. Additionally, almost 75% of couples in long-distance relationships spend up to 10 hours on the phone with each other each week, ensuring that slightly more than one-third of all respondents will regularly spend over $100 on telephone bills each month (Telocity Survey, 2001).

Couples must communicate in order to stay together. Communication is difficult for any two-earner couple—balancing work, childcare (in some cases), elder care (in other cases) and the intricacies of getting along. Distance adds a complicating factor, as documented above. Failure to communicate could mean the end of the relationship, so couples who are trying to stay together (and have quality of life as a couple) must recognize that the struggle to communicate is an added concern. As a couple whose life together has spanned the historic beginnings of e-mail use for everyone, we can attest to the money and time saving value of the Internet (Telocity, 2001)–though we still talk by phone every night! Of course, it is not the same as being together.

COMMUNITY

A large, contextual issue, related to the question of "Where is home?" is "Where is our community?" Though Homer seems to be "our home" (our legal residence and the address on all legal documents), there are consequences to that decision. These relate to such questions as "Where are our friends?" "Where do we entertain?" "Where do we do community service?" "Where do we worship?" "What is our 'community'?"

This issue of community is important. In *The Community* (1975: 3, 10), Sanders writes: "Many people today are seeking a sense of community . . . [characterized by] tradition, individualism, communality, and interdependence." He further speaks of a paradox in modern society: "as we move toward a mass society in vast metropolises, the need to maintain the strength and even to revitalize the smaller local community . . . assumes much greater importance" (1975:19). Prior to Sanders, Toennies (1957:37) speaks of the *Gemeinschaft* of communities, the "voluntary, social and reciprocal relations that are bound together by an immutable 'we-feeling'" (Foster in Porter, 1997:25). The commuting partner often has no sense of community, no "we feeling" in the Gemeinschaft sense.

Community can be defined in a number of ways: as a sense of belonging to something larger than one's self (a kind of ethnographic approach to analysis); experiencing common concern and care in a "local" setting (a sociological approach). Community is also a spatial unit (an ecological approach), often (but not always) characterized by physical proximity to others (Sanders 1975). One thing is obvious about a distance relationship–as a couple, we cannot share community except for the times we are together, nor can we "belong" to a physical community as a couple except (in our case) on weekends and college holidays.

Stuck is not as gregarious as Ware. Even if she were, her life in Oswego does not leave much time for friends. When would one entertain or "go out" with friends? Certain time commitments are necessary to maintain friendships and she has little time in Oswego to devote to that. Any aspects of community building must take place within the constraints of her work time and limited time in Oswego. Thus at Oswego any "community" Stuck has is at the college–and even that is limited by teaching at night and not being there on weekends. Stuck's situation seems to support Miller and Skeen's statement that lesbian couples who are separated because of academic responsibilities in different places experience "isolation that might not have been characteristic for a member of a married couple" (Ferber and Loeb, 1997: 121).

As a couple, some of our friends are in Homer (or the larger Cortland/ Homer area). Ware maintains some social relationships related to colleagues at her college and parishioners at our church. However, given the heavy demands on our weekends, we do not entertain much, which seems somewhat prerequisite to having friends. Both of us do some things with friends at lunch during the week, but reserve inviting friends to our home to longer vacations–Christmas, summer–and these seasonal interactions may/do affect reciprocal relationships of community.

We joined a church in Homer and attend mass there on weekends. Ware was on the school board in Homer for nine years, and has been on some other community boards and volunteer bodies; Stuck, however, is denied the opportunity to participate in such groups unless they meet only on weekends–which most do not. Since "community service" is a necessary category for promotion/tenure/discretionary increases (as well as a way to locate one's self in a community) this is a cost of Stuck's commuting. It is seen even more subtly when we go out in the community (e.g., out to dinner). Nearly everyone in town knows Ware. It is a rare dinner out when 5-6 people fail to stop by our dinner table to reacquaint themselves with Ware. If Stuck were a full time resident of the community, it is likely she would also find herself "known by everyone" (a side effect of living in a small town).

The foregoing are not unique to lesbian commuting couples, so we also need to acknowledge the difficulty of lesbians living in small towns to find "community" (if that is meant to include "like minded people") even if they lived in the same place. For us, Syracuse and Ithaca (each a 30-40 minute drive from Homer/Cortland) would be the places to go to Gay and Lesbian events (other than those sponsored by our campus Gay/Lesbian/Bisexual groups). Our ability to attend such gatherings is also limited by the amount of time we have together–sometimes the weekends (when we might attend such gatherings) are taken up with the needs of maintaining a house (as has been noted before) because we cannot do much of that during the week.

In summary, costs associated with being an academic couple in a distance relationship include existential issues: "Where is home?" "Where is community?" and not being home together. For lesbian academic couples, the added issue of "Where is our lesbian community?" may be complicated by distance as mentioned above, with the possible need to commute to (rather than live near) lesbian/gay locales and events. Other notable pragmatic issues are extra financial costs and time issues. Many of these issues would be relevant to heterosexual academic couples working in two locations also (Bruce, 1990; Wolf-Wendell et al., 2000). We would also posit that some issues of community might not be as difficult for heterosexuals–finding heterosexual others. Other couples (lesbian, gay or straight) might also have issues of children to care for; aged parents needing assistance (one of us experienced this already–again, at a distance), which might be easier if both lived in one location. Fortunately, we do not, at this time, have these responsibilities.

The foregoing addresses themes related to living as a distance couple and might be characteristic of any commuting couple. So what are themes related to the identity of academic lesbian couples?

ACADEMIC IDENTITIES: WORK TIME, MENTORING, PRODUCTIVITY

Productivity

The first distance relationship either of us knew about was that of a Cortland professor who was married to a hospital administrator in Pennsylvania. He worked hard all week, socialized little, and went to Pennsylvania on weekends. Anyone knew that you could call on him for almost any task, as long as you didn't ask him to do it over a weekend. He got work done, was a good committee member and advanced rapidly. (Sadly, finally the commuting "got to him" and he left Cortland for a lesser job in Pennsylvania.) This highlights a positive of distance relationships: with nothing to distract one in the evenings, an academic with a partner elsewhere is likely to work hard, get tasks done rapidly, and be a dependable colleague. Both Ware and Stuck are likely to work in the evenings. If we have student journals to read, we do so; if we have e-mail or listservs to monitor for classes, we do it; we prepare tests, grade papers, write academic material in the evenings. If we were in the same place, we might more likely do what we do in our times off: go shopping, go out to eat, go to a movie. (A colleague, not in a distance relationship, whose partner has just retired, is now dealing with the stressors of the expectations for play from the retired partner, so the "play" temptation is very real.)

As seen with the specific example of our male colleague, distance relationships *can* make for very successful academic productivity. "The commuting lifestyle provides the opportunity for intense concentration and more time at work by the separation of work and nonwork life" (Bunker and Zubeck, 1992: 400; Bunker and Vanderslice, 1982; Farris, 1978). Bunker, Zubeck et al. also found that "[c]ommuters were more satisfied with work life, and with the personal time available to them" and that the "gains of the commuter lifestyle are primarily in terms of personal and career development and the losses are primarily relational" (1992:405). But one must still ask: academic productivity at a distance, at what costs to the individuals and to the couple?

Mentoring and Collaboration

Mentoring is another aspect of distance relationships that can be enhanced by the partnership of two academics. When individuals are at the same campus, campus politics can be "all too much." People can tire of talking about work at home and they may have "different takes" on the same issue, which can cause rifts. In our case, Ware had been in academe for quite awhile before Stuck obtained her tenure track position. Without knowing specifics of Oswego's politics, Ware could advise, reread drafts of letters, and provide "political savvy" without sounding too much like a "know it all." In the reverse, Ware began to teach courses in Gender Issues in Education during her third decade at Cortland, and Stuck's expertise in sociology was a great help. Both of us look over each other's syllabi, check assignments for rigor, reread papers of each other's students when there are questions, and discuss pedagogy. We believe this interchange is enhanced due to our different disciplines *and* different institutions. It might seem too much like one "telling the other what to do" if we were on the same campus. In our case, the distance seems "about right" for this type of academic endeavor.

Collaboration is another plus. Because we are in different disciplines and on different campuses, there are incentives to collaboration. We have presented at, and written for, journals/conferences in both sociology and education. We have presented collaborative faculty development seminars on each other's campuses. We can apply for support from on-campus sources of funds and "multiply" the amount we receive precisely because we are on different campuses. As an added benefit of this collaboration, since we cannot be together "at home," we can travel together if we can manage to get on the same conference program, either through collaboration or individual submissions. These travel possibilities are not unique to lesbian couples, and in fact are evidence that all "[a]cademics have a great deal of control over their work schedules" (Bunker, Zubek et al., 1992; 406).

LESBIAN ACADEMIC COUPLE IDENTITY–UNIQUE ASPECTS

Hiring Policies and Practices

The foregoing suggests that in most, but not all, quality of life aspects, lesbian and heterosexual dual career commuting academics are fairly similar. However, in certain academic areas there are significant differences. As we look at colleagues and recent hires, it is abundantly clear that efforts have been, and continue to be, made to hire spouses/partners–heterosexual. Several recent studies have documented efforts by academic Vice Presidents to assist dual-career couples–generally heterosexual (Loeb, 1997; Wolf-Wendell et al., 2000; Raabe 1997). While it may be difficult for both members of a couple to find jobs at the same institution, it does happen with some frequency for heterosexuals, often with explicit institutional policy or at least practice to do so. No such practice or policy seems to exist for lesbian academics ("The Dilemma of Dual Career Couples in Academia," 1997). Clearly, many factors contribute to this, not the least of which are the lack of legal protection and fears of coming out. But for a couple known as lesbians and with solid academic reputations, this inability to secure positions on the same campus is a continual reminder of separate and unequal treatment–despite outstanding qualifications. (Of course, there is ongoing debate about the practice of spousal hiring centered around issues such as creation of special positions, exemptions made from qualifications for legitimately advertised jobs in order to hire a spouse. There is also the issue, at higher levels in academe, of the unpaid labor provided by a spouse. All these are issues needing further exploration and clarification.)

Official College Events

We may have unique opportunities to challenge assumptions by virtue of our very presence at functions: Ware had to remind her college president (some 20 years ago) that he should invite guests and "their partners" (rather than spouses), and this has become the norm over the years. We attend social functions at each of our institutions, including the inaugurations of several presidents, and (unlike some other lesbian couples we know) we acknowledge each other as partners. Only in rare cases (when we encounter someone who doesn't know either of us) do we run into interesting assumptions (e.g., that at social functions, only one individual is an academic and the other is a "spouse"). As an example, at an early social function for faculty and faculty wives, Ware was asked, "Whose wife are you?" by an older faculty spouse!

Being Out

When we began this piece, we indicated we would analyze our situation (lesbian academic couple in a distance relationship) in terms of our history, biography and culture. One thing is obvious about history—times have changed. In the early 1970s (when Ware became an academic) the gay/lesbian culture in small towns was as primitive as if Stonewall had never happened. SUNY Cortland did not have a gay/lesbian organization and a heartrending debate was held about that issue in faculty senate (with gays/lesbians being compared to "those espousing illegal acts-like a club for murderers"–statements on a handout prepared by some faculty). At that time, there was no question but that Ware would be closeted. In a gradual and painfully slow emergence, Ware has come out on her campus to numerous people/groups. She still does not come out to her classes–at least not at the beginning of a semester–finding it easier to decide her time and place situationally. Heterosexuals, single or as members of a couple, have no such fundamental identity issues with which to struggle.

Ware and Stuck often debate the wisdom of this–realizing that gay/lesbian students *need* role models! Stuck has always been "more out" but the discipline of sociology makes it a bit easier than does that of elementary education. Even Stuck's campus seems to have a more accepting culture than does Ware's. Oswego has, for instance, offered *Angels in America* as one of its theatrical presentations. Stuck has spoken at many gay and lesbian group events during her time at Oswego, more recently attending gay/lesbian end of year banquets with Ware.

State/Federal Legislation

Domestic partnership legislation took place in New York State during our years with the State University of New York. There is no real benefit to our registering for benefits under each other's policies, since we both are academics working for SUNY. However, we would register if one of us needed to be covered under the other's policies. We did applaud this change in the benefit structure. As soon as Massachusetts provided the option for registration of domestic partnerships (1993), we made sure we registered ourselves (in Provincetown during one summer vacation) and the partnership document proudly hangs on our wall. History has made it *slightly* more acceptable to be a lesbian couple than it was in 1970 when Ware began at Cortland. The current issues with gay marriage are a newer chapter in the gay rights history, and at the time of this article those issues were not resolved. We both agree that it would be nice to have the benefits that accrue to married people, and at the same time that a "marriage" would seem anticlimactic since we have been (in our minds and hearts) married since 1978–but the guarantee of state and federal civil rights and financial benefits is so very important. These are not concerns for heterosexual married couples.

CONCLUSION

A review of our histories, autobiographies, and cultures (Mills 1959) has shown that the advantages and disadvantages we have experienced through dual career commuting couplehood as lesbians are not, we feel, in many respects, appreciably different from those of heterosexual couples who work at different places. However, we do realize that policies and practices of many higher education institutions have been developed to assist the plight of the dual career heterosexual couple and do not exist to help us. We also know that colleagues and acquaintances of heterosexual academic couples in distance relationships would be sympathetic and understanding of the lack of policies and practices related to non-heterosexual academic couples. In our case, only those we choose to tell even know that we are "together," and thus living apart by virtue of our separate jobs. As in many other situations, we are assumed to be heterosexual ("old maids")–and thus, it is assumed by those who do not know us well that we are single people, living alone. Patrick Sinclair (a gay male academic) offers the following advice, "It is important to make a strong clear presence, so that people know we are there and that we contribute to society like everyone else" ("The Dilemma of Dual Career Couples in Academia," 1997). We also realize that, so far as could be determined, while there are not major "objective" differences in quality of life issues for heterosexual and lesbian academic couples, for us (and probably many, given the numbers of breakups of which we are aware) the subjective emotional costs are taking a toll after being in a commuting relationship since 1985. These are the multiple levels of reality (Berger 1963) that must be realized to help understand the life of people, specifically lesbian commuting academic couples, in historical periods (Mills).

RECOMMENDATIONS

No conclusion is sufficient without offering some recommendations for those who might be able to make changes to academic policy. First, while we are acutely aware of the problems involved, we would hope that colleges and universities would begin to develop policies to enhance the hiring of faculty members' partners, in the same way that many are making "hiring packages" for heterosexual academic couples–married or living together. Institutions of higher learning in the same general area could cooperate on this also, so that couples would not necessarily have to be at the same institution, but could certainly live in the same town. We realize implementation would require sensitivity, since all couples are not "out." However, extending the possibilities for hiring of partners certainly would be a humanistic outreach and might attract some faculty that the institution would otherwise not obtain (and retain people already hired).

Second, we would say to fellow academics, empathize with your colleagues who have distance relationships–whether they are heterosexual or gay/lesbian. Realize that these individuals are like "singles" during the week, and would enjoy invitations to dinner and chances to socialize as individuals–but at the same time realize there is a partner in absentia. Individuals and institutions could also help by providing housing assistance or "match up" services for those distance couples who have condos and homes to rent during holidays and summers. If institutions could help with such issues (like matching up visiting summer session scholars), it could make a great deal of difference.

The best assistance, however, might be the first item (even with the potential problems mentioned above). Few couples would choose to give up home and community for the sake of a job–but many do. Finding couples, gay and straight, employment in the same community, even if not at the same institution, would be the greatest benefit the institution could provide–to both the individuals and the institution!

REFERENCES

Anonymous. 1997. "My, How Times Have Changed . . . Or Have They?: A Quarter Century as a Lesbian Academic." Pp. 199-202 in Mintz, Beth and Rothblum, Esther (Eds.). 1997. *Lesbians in Academia–Degrees of Freedom.* New York: Routledge.
Berg, B. 2001. *Qualitative Research Methods for the Social Sciences.* Needham Heights, MA: Allyn & Bacon.

Berger, Peter. 1963. *Invitation to Sociology*. Garden City, NY: Anchor Books, Doubleday.

Bruce, W. 1990, March 21-24. "Dual-career couples in the university: Policies and Problems." Paper presented at the annual conference of the National Association for Women Deans, Administrators and Counselors, Nashville, TN.

Bunker, B. and Vanderslice, V.J. 1982. "Tradeoffs: Individual gains and relational losses of commuting couples." Paper presented at the American Psychological Association Convention. Washington, DC.

Bunker, B., Zubeck, J.M., Vanderslice, V.J. and Rice, R.W. "Quality of Life in Dual-Career Families: Commuting versus Single-Residence Couples." *Journal of Marriage and the Family* 54 (May 1992): 399-407.

Denzin, N.K. 1978. *The Research Act*. Chicago: Aldine.

Ferber, M.A. & J.W. Loeb (Eds.). 1997. *Academic Couples: Problems and Promises*. Urbana: University of Illinois Press.

Foster, D. 1997. "Community and Identity in the Electronic Village." Pp. 23-37 in Porter, D. 1997. *Internet Culture*. New York: Routledge.

Larson, K.H. 1992. "Economic Issues Facing Lesbian Households." Paper presented at the First Conference of the International Association for Feminist Economics, American University. Washington, DC, July 24-26.

Loeb, J.W. 1997. "Programs for academic partners: How well can they work." In M.A. Ferber & J.W. Loeb (Eds.) *Academic Couples: Problems and Promises*. Urbana: University of Illinois Press.

Long, J. 1987. "Telling women's lives: The new sociobiography." Paper presented at the annual meeting of the American Sociological Association, Chicago.

Miller, D.C. and Skeen, A. "POSSLQs and PSSSLQs: Unmarried Academic Couples" pp. 106-127 in Ferber & J.W. Loeb (Eds.) *Academic Couples: Problems and Promises*. Urbana: University of Illinois Press.

Mills, C. Wright. 1959. *The Sociological Imagination*. New York: Oxford University Press, Inc.

Mintz, Beth and Rothblum, Esther (Eds.). 1997. *Lesbians in Academia–Degrees of Freedom*. New York: Routledge.

Porter, D. 1997. *Internet Culture*. New York: Routledge.

Raabe, P.H. 1997. "Work-family policies for faculty: How 'career-and family-friendly' is academe?" In M.A. Ferber & J.W. Loeb (Eds.). *Academic Couples: Problems and Promises*. Urbana: University of Illinois Press.

Rabuzzi, Kathryn. 1982. *The Sacred and the Feminine*. New York: Seabury Press.

Sanders, I.T. 1975. *The Community*. 3rd edition. New York: Wiley & Sons.

Schneider, M. 1986. "The Relationships of Cohabiting Lesbian and Heterosexual Couples: A Comparison." *Psychology of Women Quarterly* 10 (Sept.): 234-39.

Sorcinelli, M.D. & Near, J.P. 1989. "Relations between work and life away from work among university faculty." *Journal of Higher Education*, 60:59-82.

"Telocity Survey Finds That More Than 86% Of Couples In Long-Distance Relationships Use The Internet To Keep In Touch." *Business Wire* Feb 12, 2001, p. 1040.

"The Dilemma of Dual Career Couples in Academia." 1997. *Gradvoice Online!* *www.age.uci.edu/gradvoice/97spring/couple.html*.

Toennies, F. 1957. *Community and Society*. New York: Michigan University Press.

Wolf-Wendel, Lisa; Twombly, Susan; Rice, Suzanne. "Dual Career Couples: Keeping them Together." *Journal of Higher Education* v.71, No 3 (May/June 2000): 291-321.

"Course Is Team Taught": Dimensions of Difference in Classroom Pedagogy

Patricia Lengermann

The George Washington University, Washington, DC

Jill Niebrugge

American University, Washington, DC

SUMMARY. We report on students' response to kinds of difference in the classroom as we have assessed it in our personal experience as a same-sex, mixed race, leftist couple team teaching in two disciplines and at five separate schools over a number of years. We argue that students are

---

Patricia Lengermann was born in Trinidad, educated at Oxford and Cornell Universities, and is Research Professor of Sociology at The George Washington University. She is coauthor with Jill Niebrugge of *The Women Founders: Sociology and Social Theory, 1830-1930.*

Jill Niebrugge has taught sociology and women's studies at Wells College, Gettysburg College, and the University of Iowa, and is Scholar in Residence at American University. She is coauthor with Patricia Lengermann of "Contemporary Feminist Theory" in George Ritzer and Douglas Goodman's *Sociological Theory.*

[Haworth co-indexing entry note]: "'Course Is Team Taught': Dimensions of Difference in Classroom Pedagogy." Lengermann, Patricia, and Jill Niebrugge. Co-published simultaneously in *Journal of Lesbian Studies* (Harrington Park Press, an imprint of The Haworth Press, Inc.) Vol. 9, No. 4, 2005, pp. 57-72; and: *Lesbian Academic Couples* (ed: Michelle Gibson, and Deborah T. Meem) Harrington Park Press, an imprint of The Haworth Press, Inc., 2005, pp. 57-72. Single or multiple copies of this article are available for a fee from The Haworth Document Delivery Service [1-800-HAWORTH, 9:00 a.m. - 5:00 p.m. (EST). E-mail address: docdelivery@haworthpress.com].

more accepting of differences arising out of sexual preference and race
and most resistant to differences arising out of class, especially poverty.
*[Article copies available for a fee from The Haworth Document Delivery Service:
1-800-HAWORTH. E-mail address: <docdelivery@haworthpress.com> Website:
<http://www.HaworthPress.com> © 2005 by The Haworth Press, Inc. All rights
reserved.]*

KEYWORDS. Lesbian, academic couple, team teaching, collaboration,
position sharing, mixed race

Since 1988, we have been engaged in what Auguste Comte, the puta-
tive founder of sociology, might have termed "a natural experiment"–
that is, one that occurs as part of people's daily lives in the real world
rather than in the laboratory. Our experiment–the full dimensions of
which we only realized in writing this article–arose naturally in the
course of our attempts to earn a living and has involved us in probing the
uses and meanings of difference in the college and university classroom
at five schools, in two disciplines (and several courses). Our experiment
has led us to be the proverbial canary in the mine for various kinds of
difference–that is, we have found ourselves testing the air, as it were, for
the ways people respond to different kinds of difference.

This career path is one result of our choosing a lesbian identity–
though by no means an inevitable one. In mid-life, in a moment of *folie
à deux*, much in love and full of the romantic notion of "the world well
lost," we gave up full-time jobs as tenured academics to embark on what
we saw as a life partnership as activist scholars. We were old enough to
know better but we had spent or misspent our youth in the protected
halls of academe and did not understand health insurance. We also perhaps underestimated the degree hedonism mixed with our Marxism and
led us down paths of pleasure. If Aesop were telling this, it would be the
Fable of the Marriage–or Domestic Partnership–of the Grasshoppers.
As the bills came due, we went back to teaching but kept some of our desire for togetherness by seeing if we could pick up joint appointments–
which we did.

Two principles inform this paper: organizationally, we follow the
opening conceit of a "natural experiment," dividing the paper into five
parts: *the dependent variable* (what we mean by student response to
"difference"); *the independent variable* (our presentation of difference
in the classroom); *the intervening variables* (history, schools, and

courses); *the experimental process* (the classroom experience); and, in a modification of our metaphor, *a reflection on our findings.* Analytically, in this first attempt at public autobiography, we have found ourselves using the language of sociology, our home discipline, and most particularly social theory, our academic specialty, in order to explain ourselves. This usage is not an affectation but rather the way we could most understandably tell ourselves our story. And we would predict that other papers in this volume will bear a similar disciplinary mark.

THE DEPENDENT VARIABLE

Our dependent variable, that phenomenon which changes under the impact of an external stimulus or independent variable,[1] is student response to the presentation of various kinds of difference in the classroom. In this section we define this amorphous yet very real variable–difference in the classroom.

For "difference" to exist, there needs to be in people's minds some "standard" or reference point, some "taken for granted" way of being from which one departs. For our purposes here the departure that matters is the departure from what Audre Lorde has termed *the mythical norm*: "Somewhere, on the edge of consciousness, there is what I call a *mythical norm*, . . . In america, this norm is usually defined as white, thin, male, young, heterosexual, christian, and financially secure" (Lorde 1984: 116). This norm functions in people's experience of difference as what phenomenological sociologist Alfred Schutz identifies as a "typification," a general way of naming to ourselves the essential features of experiences; typifications can range from the basic like "chair" for certain furniture, to "recipe knowledge" for how to use a computer menu, to high order cultural constructs like Lorde's mythical norm. We can operate in the daily social world, which Schutz calls "the world as taken for granted," because our typifications fit the realities we encounter. We most frequently notice our typifications when we meet situations which either violate them or, more rarely, for which we have no typification. This problem is graphically illustrated in a scene from the Kevin Kline comedy *In & Out:* a movie star returns to his ideally conventional hometown accompanied by a Hollywood starlet whom he leaves briefly at a mom and pop motel where she complains "there isn't a phone in the room" even as she stares at a standard 1950s black rotary dial model which she does not recognize, cannot typify.[2]

Thus, when we talk about difference in the classroom, we are talking about departures from significant taken for granted typifications that people use to manage their world with enough success that it does not become problematic. Difference typically occurs in the classroom as students encounter course material that is different in its typification of the world from what they have previously thought. But our focus in this paper is on the manifestation of difference that occurs when the teacher(s) departs from Lorde's mythical norm which prescribes who has most the right to power and authority in society.

THE INDEPENDENT VARIABLE

The independent variable, the stimulus that acts on the dependent variable, is that we as couple in the classroom bring at least six kinds of difference which we define here in terms of departures from taken for granted typifications.

- We team teach and share a position in a world in which students typically expect one person to be in charge, and administrators, bureaucracy–and above all, health insurance companies–typically expect a single person to hold the position.
- We are a lesbian couple in a world that privileges heterosexuality and maleness.
- We are a mixed race couple in a world that privileges whiteness and expects that couples be of the same race.
- We are couple with mixed global origins–Pat from the Caribbean and Jill from Southern California–teaching students who take U.S. experience as the standard in a world that privileges core nations.
- We are an increasingly working class couple–if one judges class in terms of how one is reimbursed–in a world that correlates authority with income.
- We are a politically identified Far Left couple in a world that takes for granted that capitalism is good and that reasonable people are centrist.

(We are also vegetarian–a difference that seems to strike some of our students as almost our most bizarre feature.)

These differences are experienced by us and presented to the students not as separate features but in the mode Black feminist sociologist Patricia Hill Collins (1998) conceptualizes as "intersectionality," the coming together in an embodied subject (or here in the embodied subjectivit*es* of a couple) of various socially constructed and distinct locations in society's hierarchies of oppression and privilege. This configuration of difference becomes apparent to the student in multiple ways. Some aspects are immediately visible: there are two instructors; Jill is "white" and Pat is a person of color, Jill sounds "American" and Pat sounds "foreign." But other differences only become apparent when and if we choose to enact them: we can choose to identify as Marxist or materialist feminist–or lesbian. And even with the ascribed characteristics, there is still a partial element of choice in the degree of relevance or emphasis that we choose to give to them.

Thus, the independent variable is shaped by our understandings–individually and jointly–of our classroom identity. Classroom identity is a subject of passionate interest for many teachers because the teacher, like the politician, the minister, and the entertainer, has as a major requisite of job performance the creation of a persona to which the viewer will grant authority, control or trust. Something of the complexity of this process is caught in Heather McHugh's (1999) "Etymological Dirge":

Calm comes from burning.
Tall comes from fast.
Comely doesn't come from come.
Person comes from mask.

In the ongoing dynamics of the classroom, the teacher experiences with particular force the process which sociologists understand as the ongoing construction of the self. That process, outlined in its classic statement by George Herbert Mead, turns on *taking the role of the other*. Mead argues that the self is a social product, arising out of our learning in socialization that we are an object to other people and that we can imagine how we appear to those others–to *particular others*, that is individual people, and to what he sees as the referent for the unitary self, *a generalized other*, a synthesis of what we believe to be the understandings of a whole community. Mead does not pursue the problems and possibilities of bringing together numerous generalized others. But the classroom teacher's experience may be just that: an attempt to hold together the viewpoints of many particular others–students, colleagues and administrators–and a complex of generalized others, her understandings of the expectations of her significant communities of reference, including but not limited to the scholarly community of her discipline.

The concept of the generalized other is a way we talk through our different understandings of the self as we develop a consensus identity of who we must be as we enter the classroom. Jill has always been rather fond of the concept because to a significant degree she has lived an American life–white, economically secure, Christian; what she was asked to learn in school she could learn and made sense to her; her major experience of difference was that her parents were committed liberal Democrats in a Republican county during the years of HUAC and Eisenhower. This primary socialization has left her with a sense that one can anchor selfhood in a generalized understanding of a community's expectations, though she would now be hard put to apply a single name to hers–can one be a radical materialist feminist Unitarian Stoic?

Pat's life experience leads her to question the universality of Mead's theory of a generalized other. She grew up in the economically poor, racially mixed, multicultural island world of Trinidad and Tobago, in an emotionally secure but economically precarious single-parent home; an Anglican in a world where Christianity was one faith among many, and a student at an academically rigorous school of the British colonial/missionary tradition. She early found it "natural" to become the various persons expected of her as she moved among these multiple distinct social settings. Like Jill she could do successfully the academic work expected of her, an ability which got her to the world of North American academia as an adult. She understands her performance as a classroom teacher as the interpretation of one significant role, among many, that she must seem to perform easily by calling upon her repertoire of personae to configure herself as situations seem to demand. Behind those various masks, she experiences herself as the critical observer, the identified and self identified "stranger," loyal to the intimates in her life and to the body of knowledge which is her profession.

For both of us our academic socialization was to the generalized other of a community of scholars that was Ivory Tower and masculine: a generalized other that spoke in that internal conversation of the self of "value neutrality," "scholarly objectivity," "fair play," "established canons," "classic texts." That original generalized other of the community of scholars was vastly modified for us, as for many, by feminism and other liberationist movements of the end of the twentieth century. The feminist generalized other spoke of "political engagement," "the personal as political," "respect for situated vantage points," and "marginalized voices," and it changed the way we interpreted and enacted the role of professor.

What we have come to do over time in planning a class is to agree on what Schutz calls our "in-order-to motives," that is, we say to ourselves, "We are teaching this class in order to . . ." Three motives are particularly important. One is pragmatic self-interest: we are teaching this class in order to earn a living; some classes go badly occasionally (and a few go badly from day one) but we find a solace in telling ourselves at the end of a day or semester that we have met one primary goal–to keep body and soul together. Our second in-order-to motive has as a referent the "mainstream" community of scholars in our discipline: we are teaching in order to "cover" the material, that is, to give the student the ideas and tools generally agreed to be the subject of the course. Our third in-order-to-motive taps our sense of ourselves as critical thinkers, as activist intellectuals, and as members of oppressed communities whose open presence as teachers in the classroom has only been made possible by the struggles of earlier generations. Thus, we design the course in order to let the student engage with issues of inclusivity and social justice. This final in-order-to motive produces an ongoing tension among our wish to be fair to the content we teach, to respect the student's independent subjectivity and to give faithful answer to the question, "What the hell are we doing in this classroom if we are not raising issues of social justice?"

INTERVENING VARIABLES

Three factors intervene in our presentation of self in the classroom: history, the character of the school, and the content of the courses.

History. Since we first taught a course together in 1985, the United States, while growing much more conservative on social issues like welfare rights and class stratification, has granted more acknowledgment to the fact that there are gay people in the world–even creating "positive" portrayals with "lesbian chic" and "metrosexuals." Biographically, we may have been advantaged by these shifts as colleges sought diversity in their faculty by race and sexual orientation–at least in their temporary faculty. Further, we have been selective in the jobs we have sought, focusing on the Northeast and Middle Atlantic states with one period at a Midwestern state university singled out nationally as a leader in affirmative action. We have never applied to teach in the

South or Southwest. Our one venture into the Rocky Mountains was met with a chillingly quick rejection when, for a job for which we were extremely well qualified, we sent an inquiry to see if they would consider hiring a couple and got the reply (practically by return e-mail) that "we do not like team teaching." Since it seems to us that team teaching is something a faculty might "question" or "have reservations about" but not "like" or "dislike," we assume that what was not "liked" was us as a couple.

Schools. We have held temporary (from a semester to three years) shared appointments at a variety of schools which we profile in Table 1 in terms of qualities that would affect how students might experience us: demographics of the institution–size, location, fiscal base; diversity of student body in the courses we taught (sociology and women's studies); institutional orientation to difference.

Courses. We have team taught in two areas, sociology and women's studies, disciplines which have as part of their subject matter social change and critique. Within these disciplines, we have taught technical, specialized courses such as theory and methods, substantive and descriptive courses such as sociology of gender or women's activism, and broad-based general education requirements like American society and introduction to women's studies.

THE CLASSROOM EXPERIENCE

In the classroom, team teaching, we present difference in two major ways: one, as embodied subjects, and two, as course content where it may appear as diversity, inequality or critique.

The first manifestation is when we enter the classroom on the first day–there are two of us instead of one; we are mixed race, and, as soon as we speak, we reveal different global origins from each other.

The second is as we go over the syllabus. The lead item "How to Contact Instructors" makes apparent that we are not only team teaching but that we are a couple–we tell the students how to call us at home. The course requirements acknowledge that students may also be juggling several identities which affect the terms under which they are present in the classroom by formalizing flexibility with policies like the "personal leave coupon" (an idea from the listserv for Sociologists for Women in Society) which the student can use without elaboration to submit an assignment late. This concern with flexibility reflects our need for some bending of requirements to make our work lives possible. The syllabus

TABLE 1. Schools and Classroom Diversity

School/ Courses Taught	Institutional Profile	Student Diversity in Classes We Taught*	Institutional Concern with Diversity
Berne/ Women's Studies	private, coed liberal arts; 2500 students; small city in rural Northeast; endowment and tuition	high–economic class; good–race and global location; fair–sexual orientation; low–gender	divided faculty–inclusivity versus classic tradition; some willingness to accommodate with material resources non-traditional hires
Private U/ Sociology	private liberal arts university with professional schools; 5000 students; major Mid-Atlantic metropolis; intensely tuition driven	high–global location; good–gender; fair–race; low–economic class, sexual orientation	administration focused on goal of "global university," counts foreign students as minority representation, cutting programs with high non-traditional student enrollment; tolerates non-traditional hires but does nothing to facilitate
Stanton/ Sociology; Women's Studies	private, women's liberal arts; 400 students; rural Northeast; well endowed, money for scholarships	high–sexual orientation; good–economic class; fair–race and global location	divided faculty committed to diversity versus concern for "diminution of standards"; unwilling to spend money necessary to provide for non-traditional appointments
State U/ Sociology; Women's Studies	state flagship; 28,000 students; city of 65,000 in rural Midwest setting; state taxes; low tuition	high–economic class; fair–global location, sexual orientation; low (reflects state demographics)–race	forces for diversity and progressive programming in control; very welcoming and accommodating of non-traditional hires
Union/ Women's Studies; Sociology	private, coed liberal arts; 2500 students; small town (7000) in Mid-Atlantic state 3 hours from major metropolitan areas; tuition driven	high–gender; low–economic class, race, global location, sexual orientation–95% white, heterosexual business class, U.S.	administration divided: old guard in admissions and recruitment sought homogeneity while new guard in faculty hires very welcoming and accommodating of non-traditional hires

*"High" means about 1/4 or more; good means about 1/5; fair, about 1/6 to 1/10; low, less than 1/10.

overview also makes clear that the course content balances traditional coverage with innovations designed to make the course more inclusive and focused on social justice. For instance, in sociological theory, we balance the mainstream canon, created out of white elite class male experience, with theories created out of the experiences of women, racial minorities, gays and lesbians and working class people.

A way difference is present is in lectures and class discussion. For instance, we use our revision of the theory canon to show students how difference matters in the formulation of theory: if these "new" figures are to be understood in terms of their social placement, then the "founding fathers" are also to be so understood, as men located in a nexus of social privilege. Further, in a theory class, where one needs to illustrate abstract concepts with concrete examples, we draw on our everyday life experiences shaped by the consequences of difference. Thus, talking about Chrys Ingraham's concept of "heteronormativity," we mention how encountering a heterosexual couple on a path too narrow for four abreast, we and they habitually enact the assumption that same sex should defer to heterosex. Or, discussing "white privilege," we talk about its subtle manifestations as a waiter offers Jill the wine to taste though Pat has placed the order.

Our use of difference in lecture and discussion involves not only our shared departures from the mythical norm but differences between us as individuals. So, we debate the significance of a concept, showing that we each relate to it differently, as in the case of Mead's concept of the generalized other and the unitary self, explaining much as we have done above, why that concept would work for Jill and not for Pat, offering alternative conceptualizations such as W.E.B. DuBois's "double consciousness," and asking students to situate themselves in relationship to these alternatives. This act of situating themselves in relation to a theoretical concept is training in the all-important intellectual skill of being able to differentiate between what a thinker has argued and how you personally feel about that argument.

A final way difference is present is in the dynamics potentially common to all team teaching–at least if the teachers are typically together in the classroom. The major dynamic is that we alternate roles: "task leader" and "emotional manager," passionate critic and moderating voice, earnest claim maker and humorous debunker. Another dynamic is in our ability to establish relationships with different types of students based on the students' perceptions of who we are.

REFLECTIONS ON OUR FINDINGS

Our purpose in this section is to measure our effectiveness, that is, how well we have moved students towards thinking about difference in terms of some standard of social justice, of "a world . . . that can be partially shared and that is friendly to earthwide projects of finite freedom" (Haraway, 1988: 578). In assessing our effectiveness, we begin from our two most general findings: (1) that thus far our authority in the classroom has not been affected by our differences combined or taken as separate pieces and (2) that students have a range of responses to difference, more complex than the logical continuum from hostility to neutrality to acceptance, as we depict in Figure 1. The rest of this discussion focuses on the factors that shape these responses and on our effectiveness as a factor either as embodied subjects or through actions structuring course content.

Our most humbling findings is the strength of the intervening variables. One of the hardest things to face in classroom teaching is the fact that one is responsible for only a small part of what occurs–the teacher/student dynamic is not a 50/50 split. The makeup of the student body in terms of embodied difference and political orientation is a critical intervening variable in the response to difference in the classroom. The number of minority students–by race, sexual orientation, class, or global location–is a powerful influence in getting mainstream students to engage seriously with issues of difference. Equally important are students' political orientations, their thoughts and feelings about the workings and implications of social power. Our reflections lead us to identify six kinds of political orientation (see Table 2). The non-reflected upon worldview–in all three of its substantive forms–may exist independent of any structured understanding and is brought by the student from their family of origin where it is acquired not through formal instruction but through a natural identification with the ethos of the home–its conversations, its ambience, its relevances. This deep and early habituation is the posture one feels safe in, reassured by its loca-

FIGURE 1. Responses to Difference

```
                            /   discomfort-------hostility
indifference---------neutrality----affect
                        *           \
   tacit  acceptance              concern-------support-------embrace
```

TABLE 2. Student Political Orientations

non-reflective conservative wordview	non-reflective liberal worldview	non-reflective apolitical worldview
reflective conservative philosophy	reflective liberal philosophy	reflective apolitical mindset

tion in all one's feeling memories of the home; one's return to it produces what Bourdieu (1984: 3) terms "an enchanted experience." Bourdieu is writing about "taste" and aesthetics; but if we are right in applying his thinking to political orientations, it may help explain the capacity of students to persevere in certain attitudes despite evidence and pressure to the contrary. The reflected upon worldview–in all three substantive forms–may have come to the student in some measure from the home, but as a learned, not natural, understanding. The classroom experience may help students move to work out more systematically what they believe–and why–about social power and by extension, justice; but in our experience we–and teachers generally–rarely bring about permanent change in political orientation, in part because the material interests that produced an orientation in the family continue to shape the student's life after graduation.

Student response is also affected by type of course: the greater the degree of specialized knowledge, the more openness there is both to us as different and to course content about difference, perhaps because students recognize that they cannot navigate the program without mastering the skills we seem expert in. In introductory classes the generality of course content combined with the student's casual relationship to it reduces our authority as experts. This variation is not a result of student maturation; it holds true when seniors take an introductory level course or when a lower division student enrolls in an upper division course.

The strength of these intervening variables is a constant in the conclusions that follow.

Our presence as embodied subjects serves to normalize some aspects of difference, most particularly that of a lesbian couple. This normalization of lesbian identity particularly positively affects lesbian or questioning students. Its effect on heterosexuals varies by their political orientation–for liberal students, we are probably only an elaboration of a type; for apolitical students, we may be a surprise that leads to further thinking; for conservative students, we may be simply an "exception" to a general understanding of deviant behavior. We have noticed–as compared with previous experience teaching alone and not publicly out–a disappearance of intentionally homophobic comments in class. Nor do we get blatantly homophobic comments on evaluations–though comments against team teaching or "too many personal examples" may be covert signals of homophobia.

This response may be explained in several ways. One is that changes in the larger society have rendered homophobia less acceptable *for the students in the courses we teach at the schools where we teach*. A second interpretation is that the students simply do not want to confront us on this issue because they like us even if they disapprove of who we are; they are afraid of our penalizing them, or they think it rude to make a personal attack. Against this interpretation is the fact of students' willingness to disagree about other points of difference that we embody, such as race. Further, students do make comments that show unconscious homophobia, most frequently explaining people's behaviors in terms of "not wanting to be thought gay."

Our normalization is empowering to some lesbian students who have been passed over by other instructors because of their unconventionality or to students sorting through identities of which lesbian is one part. At State U, our best theory student proved to be a lesbian in her midtwenties, in a long-term relationship, who was majoring in another field when she enrolled in our large lecture theory class. Her presentation of self was so androgynous that for the first weeks we were uncertain about her gender (and frequently discussed our "need to know" in terms of theories we teach about the gender identity and social distance). She changed majors to sociology on the basis of our course and went on to graduate work on a full fellowship, and has told us directly how much it mattered to have someone who was "different like her." Similarly, a Mormon student at Stanton College who, while questioning the doctrines of the church, was devoted to her family heritage of strong Mormon pioneer women, found us and the theories we taught useful in bringing together being Mormon with being lesbian.

We were least useful to students who defined sexual orientation or gender identity as their core self. This included transgender students and students who were focused on issues of sexual expression such as masturbation and sadomasochism. These students often see us as rather tame–and not very sexy–representatives of their concerns.

In terms of course content, we have found that student responses vary with the types of difference we address. Race (and possibly by extension global location) is most frequently responded to as a difference that deserves acceptance; sexual orientation is responded to as a difference that deserves either acceptance or neutrality; class is far and away most frequently responded to with hostility.

Our greatest effectiveness in communicating course content about difference has been in the teaching of African American social theory–in courses at all levels about sociological theory. There we do pioneering work incorporating classical feminist and African American theories into courses which typically deal only with the work of white men. Without exception the students, regardless of background, are interested in these theories, especially African American theory. Feminist theory is a harder sell, especially in a coed setting, perhaps because it is construed by many students to divide men and women–despite our sustained attempt to show it as a general argument for social justice for both women and men. African American social theory–also presented as a general theory for social analysis and social justice–does not threaten the heterosexual relationships the students are, for the most part, developing, and seems, for the many students who understand it, to offer useful explanations of parts of their life.

Further, we found that indifference could exist side-by-side with tacit endorsement: students could pay lip service to equal rights but not muster the energy to care actively about the persons to whom those rights were to be extended–whatever they were. One example may illustrate this phenomenon: Teaching a feminist essay collection, *Listen Up,* we have, by voting with three or four black students, managed to get the class to select for discussion "Betrayal Feminism," Veronica Chambers' account of her experience as a black student with white feminists who (among other things) failed to do the reading when a black feminist writer was assigned. But when it came time for discussion, we discovered that white students committed in principle to racial equality had not gotten the essay read.

In course content, we have been least effective offering a Marxist critique of class inequality. The most unabashed expression of hostility to difference we encounter everywhere we teach–though by no means from every student or in every class–is to the poor. Excepting in the main the students in sociological theory, we are told repeatedly that "poor people should not have children"; if necessary, they should not have sex; and that they deserve their fate because they are "uneducated," "lazy," "immoral," or "irresponsible." Particularly marked is the sense that poor people are where they are because they do not work hard–and this comes from students like a Private U senior who is going home to inherit the family undertaking business. The one area of concession is that most students argue for greater educational opportunity for "really bright poor children"–presumably average poor children deserve their fate. These attitudes persist despite our supplying reams of census data and analyses of the dual labor market.

Why? Several answers suggest themselves. One may be that the poor cannot be easily made into an "exotic" manifestation of "difference." They always have to be related in not very flattering ways to our own condition, the rights we claim, the social system in which we all live. Further, the poor, unlike lesbians and gays, have no parts of their community with the resources to mount counter-publicity campaigns, run for Congress, or argue the meaning of being poor in postmodernist academic treatises. Another part of the explanation is that poor or blue collar students, typically and understandably in such an atmosphere, stay invisible and closeted; they do not present themselves as fellow students with life issues that their classmates should take seriously. A further fact is that while the students directly confront us as an embodied lesbian mixed-race couple, they do not see us as poor–even when we are much less well off than they; therefore, attacks on the poor are not construed as attacks on us. Finally, there is a fairly direct correlation between attitudes toward the poor and the general economic class of the students at various schools. Berne is the exception, drawing students from affluent but liberal families; Stanton and State U have significant representation of students from blue collar and poor families and are muted in their hostility to the poor; Union and Private U, which draw students from affluent apolitical or conservative families, were where we encountered the most hostility to our teaching about poverty and inequality.

CONCLUSION

Thus, we, like Gibson, Marinara and Meem (2000: 92-93), have found that "It is not enough for teachers merely to include in their curricula readings about race, class, gender, and sexuality, for the traditional inclusion model fails to challenge the academic mindset that assumes the centrality of white, middle-class, male, heterosexual values and desires." To this we would add, as a last note from the canary in the mine, that difference as a departure from the mythical norm continues to be a way society organizes to justify injustice and that to combat this we must not only change students' attitudes toward difference, we must give them space in which to think about what they mean and wish the society to mean by "justice."

NOTES

1. In classical experimental design, one is, of course, in theory able to specify rigidly limited independent and dependent variables; that is not the case with the "natural experiment" where one may have complex independent, dependent and intervening variables.

2. At least two points for contemporary lesbian existence flow from this understanding of the function of typification in people's experience of the world. Phenomenologically, one importance of lesbian couples being publicly out is that the more we are present, the more people have a typification of us and therefore we are not a source of "strangeness," which is in itself a problem for people no matter how they might come to feel about the "strangeness." A second phenomenological point is that the more of us there are, the more the typification becomes nuanced, allowing room for perceptions of individuals. In other words, it is a typification and a stereotype.

REFERENCES

Bourdieu, Philip. 1984. *Distinction*. New York: Routledge and Kegan Paul.

Collins, Patricia Hill. 1998. *Fighting Words: Black Women and the Search for Justice*. Minneapolis: University of Minnesota Press.

Gibson, Michelle, Martha Marinara, and Deborah Meem. 2000. "Bi, Butch, and Bar Dyke: Pedagogical Performances of Class, Gender and Sexuality." *College Composition and Communication* 52:1/September: 69-94.

Haraway, Donna. 1988. "Situated Knowledge: The Science Question in Feminism and the Privilege of Partial Perspective." *Feminist Studies* 14: 575-600.

Ingraham, Chrys. 1998. *White Weddings*. NY: Routledge.

Lorde, Audre. 1984. *Sister Outsider*. Trumansburg, NY: Crossings Press.

McHugh, Heather. 1999. *The Father of the Predicaments*. NY: Villard.

Mead, George Herbert. 1934/1962. *Mind, Self and Society*. Chicago: U of Chicago Press.

Schutz, Alfred. 1967. *The Phenomenology of the Social World*. Evanston: Northwestern University Press.

Schutz, Alfred and Thomas Luckmann. 1973. *The Structures of the Life-World*. Evanston: Northwestern University Press.

Dual-Career Queer Couple Hiring in Southwest Virginia: Or, the Contract That Was Not One

Shelli B. Fowler
Karen P. DePauw

Virginia Polytechnic Institute, Blacksburg, VA

SUMMARY. Although dual-career hires are a common recruitment tool in academe, they remain a challenge for institutions hiring same-sex couples. This narrative tells the story of one such couple–it focuses on our professional and personal journey and the collective social activism

---

Shelli B. Fowler is Director of the Graduate Education Development Institute (GEDI) in Learning Technologies and Associate Professor of English at Virginia Tech. She earned her PhD from The University of Texas at Austin. Her research areas include critical pedagogy, African American literature, and the integration of teaching, learning, and technologies. She is the co-editor of *Included in English Studies: Learning Climates That Cultivate Racial and Ethnic Diversity* and the recipient of several teaching awards.

Karen P. DePauw is Vice Provost for Graduate Studies and Dean of the Graduate School at Virginia Tech and tenured Professor in the Departments of Sociology and Human Nutrition, Foods & Exercise. She earned the AB in sociology from Whittier College, MS in special education from California State University, Long Beach, and a PhD in kinesiology from Texas Woman's University. Her research focuses on disability studies and sport science. Her most recent book is *Disability Sport.*

[Haworth co-indexing entry note]: "Dual-Career Queer Couple Hiring in Southwest Virginia: Or, the Contract That Was Not One." Fowler, Shelli B., and Karen P. DePauw. Co-published simultaneously in *Journal of Lesbian Studies* (Harrington Park Press, an imprint of The Haworth Press, Inc.) Vol. 9, No. 4, 2005, pp. 73-88; and: *Lesbian Academic Couples* (ed: Michelle Gibson, and Deborah T. Meem) Harrington Park Press, an imprint of The Haworth Press, Inc., 2005, pp. 73-88. Single or multiple copies of this article are available for a fee from The Haworth Document Delivery Service [1-800-HAWORTH, 9:00 a.m. - 5:00 p.m. (EST). E-mail address: docdelivery@haworthpress.com].

Available online at http://www.haworthpress.com/web/JLS
doi:10.1300/J155v9n04_06

that challenged one university to begin to address issues that face LGBT
faculty throughout higher education. *[Article copies available for a fee from
The Haworth Document Delivery Service: 1-800-HAWORTH. E-mail address:
<docdelivery@haworthpress.com> Website: <http://www.HaworthPress.
com> © 2005 by The Haworth Press, Inc. All rights reserved.]*

KEYWORDS. Lesbian, academic couple, spousal hiring, domestic
partner benefits

Dual-career couple hires inside academe have become a routine recruitment tool, particularly in the case of administrative hires and especially when the institution is located in a rural or non-urban area. What
is not yet routine practice in many institutions of higher education, however, is the application of those same recruitment tools for dual-career,
same-sex couples. In 2002, as an academic dual-career, same-sex couple we experienced firsthand what we viewed, and what many within
academe viewed, as hiring discrimination on the basis of our sexual orientation at Virginia Polytechnic Institute and State University (Virginia
Tech). Although our experience began as emblematic of the kind of discriminatory practices that lesbian, gay, bisexual, and transgender faculty, staff, and administrators may too often have to confront, its
resolution works to remind us all about the importance and significance
of collective action in making social change.
  Because there is currently no federal legislation to protect against
employment discrimination on the basis of sexual orientation or gender
identity–The Employment Non-Discrimination Act, or ENDA, has not
yet been passed by Congress–there is ample opportunity for employers,
including colleges and universities across the nation, to deny LGBT
employees jobs and/or promotions on the basis of sexual orientation
without much worry about legal repercussions. While such discrimination
likely occurs at institutions of higher education more often than we would
like to think, it is very difficult to prove, as very few employers overtly declare their heterosexist actions to be such. Instead, homophobia in academe
most often "strikes in closed-door meetings of tenure-review and
promotion committees and in secret letters of recommendation" and that
"[r]ejection and denial are almost always attributed to the victim's al-
leged personal and intellectual shortcomings" (Esther Newton, cited in
Steward 2003, p. 33). Although most states do not have non-discrimination legislation, many universities, including Virginia Tech, have

broadly inclusive non-discrimination policies that prohibit firing and/or harassment on the basis of sexual orientation. Yet since the stated reason for not hiring or not promoting an LGBT staff or faculty member is rarely officially declared to be connected to sexual orientation, few of us are able to challenge directly any perceived discriminatory action on the basis of sexual orientation via an institution's non-discrimination policy. Still, the importance of a broadly inclusive non-discrimination policy at an institution of higher education should not be overlooked. The way in which such a policy affects the university's climate is substantial. While the existence of a policy may not prevent discrimination from occurring, the lack of a policy altogether can implicitly send a chilling message about the campus climate for diversity.

Many institutions of higher education have progressive recruitment and retention policies to further their diversity goals. Some, however, are not so progressive. Some perpetuate either directly or indirectly what Adrienne Rich (1983) so aptly named "compulsory heterosexuality." In a compulsory heterosexual worldview, there is a lack of understanding that all sexuality is always already public. In fact, there is a common misunderstanding that LGBT folks force their sexuality into the public arena whenever they talk about cultural practices and legal policies that discriminate against LGBT individuals or couples. In other words, the prevailing cultural misconception is that sexuality is private and that LGBT individuals inappropriately put sexuality into the open when they are "out." Likewise, those who support the current deluge of proposed marriage-protection laws in several state legislatures do not see such laws as redundant; instead, they tend to see non-discriminatory legislation that would guarantee equal protection to same-sex couples under the law as "special rights" legislation. Greta Gaard argues that such "cultural heterosexism" infuses all levels of our legal, religious, academic, health, and media systems.

> The liberal dichotomy of public and private serves to obscure the fact that heterosexuality is very public–billboards, media, retail shops all cater to the sealing of heterosexual relationships, while gays and lesbians are supposed to keep our sexuality "private." But anti-lesbian harassment occurs in very public places–in the classroom, the faculty lounge, in journals and publications, in promotion and tenure hearings, as well as on the streets. It is time to make some of these "private" stories public. (Gaard, 1996, p. 120)

With the intent of helping to increase awareness about LGBT discrimination issues in higher education, we would like to share the personal and private story of our own very public dual-career couple hire.

ADVENTURES AT VIRGINIA TECH

Our adventure at Virginia Tech occurred in 2002, and our version of this adventure is, of course, a personal narrative that is based on our own views and interpretation of events. Virginia Tech is a large land-grant, research university located in a small college town at the foot of the Blue Ridge Mountains in Southwest Virginia. Historically, Tech began as an all-white, all-male institution with a large and active Core of Cadets. According to several accommodated spouses at our institution, dual-career couple hires (or spousal-accommodation hires) have been standard issue at Virginia Tech for quite some time. Although there has been no official policy governing the practice, there does appear to have been a *de facto* practice that has sanctioned spousal-accommodation hires over the years–at least for straight, white, legally married couples.

In the fall of 2001, Karen P. DePauw was nominated for inclusion in the pool of applicants for the nationally advertised position of Vice Provost for Graduate Studies and Dean of the Graduate School at Virginia Tech. At that time, Karen was the Dean of the Graduate School at Washington State University, and Shelli B. Fowler was an Associate Professor with a joint appointment in English and Comparative Ethnic Studies at WSU. Karen agreed to apply and our adventure with Tech began. By February of 2002, Karen was one of the finalists for the position, and she was flown in for a week-long, on-site interview that included a trip to Tech's Northern Virginia locations in Falls Church and Alexandria in addition to her presentation and interviews at the Blacksburg campus. In March, the Provost told Karen that she was the candidate Tech wanted to hire and invited her to return to Tech for a second visit. We already knew that Tech included sexual orientation in its non-discrimination policy, as that was one of the important factors in our seriously considering Tech. It was at that point, as part of the initial negotiations, that Karen asked if Virginia Tech had a partner-accommodation policy. The Provost assured her that yes, Tech indeed understood the necessity of accommodating spouses and partners, and when Karen discussed the kind of academic position that her female partner currently held and would be interested in exploring at Tech, there was not a discernible moment of hesitation, nor apparently even an eyelash batted by the Provost as the possible options for Shelli were discussed.

By mid-March, we had both visited Virginia Tech. As Karen met for the second time with central administration and others, Shelli interviewed with the Department of English. It was important to discover if Shelli was a good fit for Tech's English department, and during a short interview with the department's administrators, as well as in a large interview setting with 15 or 20 faculty members, she had the opportunity, as did the department, to see if there was a good match. We also explored Blacksburg and surroundings in an attempt to determine whether we felt like we could be active contributors to both the university and Blacksburg communities. Nothing in our visit to Tech suggested anything of the events to come. Everyone with whom we met in the university community as well as in the Blacksburg community was friendly and welcoming. The fact that we were a same-sex couple did not seem to be an issue.

Shortly after Shelli's interviews, the English Department reviewed her materials in more depth, discussed her suitability, and voted to approve her candidacy as a tenured member of their department. Following that confirmation, the Provost offered each of us a contract. We discussed it further and decided to accept, sent two signed contracts back to the Provost during the last week in March, and planned to join the Virginia Tech community in August 2002.

But not so fast. . . . What we thought (and no doubt what many thought) to be a routine senior administrative hire was not acceptable to some individual (or small handful of individuals) who apparently took it upon him or herself or themselves to try to abort a process that had followed Tech's standard operating procedures for an administrative hire (and "spousal" hire). In early April, Karen received a hateful e-mail, sent anonymously from a remailer program that hides the sender's e-mail address, identity, and location. The cowardly sender told Karen that we would not be welcome at Tech and that she shouldn't take the job. The e-mail provided links to Websites detailing the September 23, 2000, murder of Danny Overstreet, a gay man in Roanoke (less than an hour from Blacksburg), implying that such could be our fate should we move here. At the time, we chose to ignore the e-mail. We decided not to empower the sender by taking it seriously or by investing any energy in acknowledging or responding to the e-mail.

In May 2002, at the end of the spring term, we returned to Blacksburg to look for a place to live. Karen also met again with the Provost, and other administrators, as well as the Interim Dean of the Graduate

School. Shelli met with the chair of the English department. She was shown which office she would have (complete with her new computer sitting in its box in the corner of the office), and reviewed sample syllabi for the courses she would begin teaching in August. The guidelines for textbook orders were discussed, and she was looking forward to working with her new colleagues. Shelli was welcomed as a new member of the department, and no suggestion was made by anyone that we would not be welcomed here.

As we were later to learn, some time late in the spring semester another hateful and homophobic e-mail was sent to only selected members of the Board of Visitors, Virginia Tech's governing board, part of whose responsibilities includes ratifying faculty appointments. Apparently, this e-mail was also sent by an anonymous remailer that hides the identity of the sender. It apparently named Shelli as Karen's lesbian partner, and went on in a homophobic diatribe against our hires. And unfortunately, but not, we'd argue, coincidentally, the e-mail was selectively sent to the handful of conservative members of the Board of Visitors.

At the June 3, 2002, quarterly meeting of the Board, our names, along with some nine other faculty hires, were on the Faculty Personnel Changes Report to be ratified. According to the minutes of the Academic Affairs Committee (the sub-committee of the Board that handles initial ratification of new personnel), that committee approved all of the recommendations of the Faculty Personnel Changes Report, as it typically does (Report of the Academic Affairs Committee, 2002). Our understanding is that during the Academic Affairs Committee meeting on June 3, 2002, everything went as it ordinarily does; that is, there was no discussion of any of the new hires on the list, including our appointments. Interestingly, if there had been any concern (from procedural to budgetary issues), the Academic Affairs Committee is one of the groups within the Board committee structure that would be ordinarily responsible for raising such concern about any hires. Again, the Academic Affairs Committee had no issue with any hire on the list.

During the Board of Visitors' closed session later that afternoon, however, things were not, apparently, business as usual. Senior administrators, including the President and Provost, were asked to leave the meeting, which is, we've been told, very unusual. At the end of what was close to a three-hour session, the Board emerged to reconvene in public session. Regarding the closed session items for salary and personnel actions, it was announced that "unanimous approval was given to the *Resolution for the Ratification of the Personnel Changes Report* with one change as considered in Closed Session" (Minutes, 2002, p. 9). All of the hires on the list were approved, except for one–Shelli B. Fowler's. No explanation was offered.

The Provost called us on the morning of June 4th, 2002, to inform us of the Board's action, but he could not tell us why my contract was nullified. No one seemed able or willing to explain. In fact, it was a full two months after the decision, in August 2002, that the Board issued what has been called a "terse statement blaming the budget" (Bartlett, 2002, p. A12).

It is certainly true that Tech was wrestling with a serious budget crisis. But it has always seemed to us that if *that* were truly the reason for taking Shelli's name off of the approved hires list, then a rationale and criteria for the process could have easily accompanied the Board decision, at least to the President and Provost and the department chair of English. Instead, the silence spokes volumes . . . to us, and to concerned faculty, staff, and students here at Virginia Tech, who were taken aback and outraged by the decision. As news about the anonymous anti-gay e-mail that had been sent to the Board made the rounds, folks became increasingly suspicious about the Board's motives. The fact that the money for Shelli's line had already been allotted also made it a bit odd that the Board would decide that Tech could not afford to hire her. Further, the Board of Visitors had routinely and without incident approved a spousal accommodation hire for a straight couple three months earlier. The spouse was hired into a tenure-track faculty position under the aegis of the same budget constraint and the spouse's contract was ratified without any questions or concerns at the March 2002 Board of Visitors meeting. It was this fact that led many in the Virginia Tech community to believe that homophobia, rather than the budget, drove the decision to nullify Shelli's contract. (The Board would also do spousal hires for two additional Deans nine months and one year after our hire.)

We became personally convinced that the budget issue was not the real reason that Shelli's contract had not been approved in the *pro forma* way that faculty contracts are ordinarily approved after we read about the Rector of the Board of Visitors' response to a question posed by a *Chronicle of Higher Education* reporter in late September. When the Rector was asked if he could assure faculty members at Tech that the decision to nullify Shelli's contract did not reflect anti-gay bias, as many believed it did, he declined to do so. That's right. He declined to do so. The reporter later told Shelli that he asked the Rector that question three times because he was so surprised that the Rector was willing to suggest, at least indirectly via his refusal to declare otherwise, that homophobia, that an "anti-gay bias" apparently did indeed drive the decision (Bartlett, 2002, p. A12).

You might, at this point, be wondering why we decided to come to Virginia Tech at all. It is a reasonable question. Our initial response was not a positive one, and we momentarily considered not coming to Tech. But it soon became clear to both of us that if we did not come to Tech, if we did not fight against what appeared very clearly to us to be discrimination, the Board would succeed in aborting Karen's hire, thereby overturning the hiring process following a competitive national search, and the message that would be sent to the Virginia Tech community and beyond was that gays and lesbians were not welcome at this institution of higher education. We both work for social justice and equity in our separate academic areas, so it was now time, as issues of social justice came home in a very personal way, to stand up for diversity. In addition, it was also clear to us that Karen's contract had not been nullified, and Karen had been hired via a national, competitive search process to lead the Graduate School in Tech's efforts to become a Top 30 research institution. We felt, on some level, that a line had been drawn in the sand by a very small handful of closed-minded individuals on the Board, and not only was it important that Karen fulfill her contract, but that we couldn't ignore the larger ramifications and just remain comfortably ensconced in the accepting community at Washington State University–ultimately, we agreed that we would come to Tech and work with others here for positive change.

Now, as dismal and depressing as all this may sound, there is a good side to this story, a very positive and upbeat part of this adventure. And that is that we were not alone in this struggle against discrimination. One of the factors supporting our decision to come to Blacksburg to work for change at Virginia Tech was the immediate and overwhelmingly supportive response to us by the larger Tech community. From the central administration to undergraduate students (faculty, staff, students, and community members), there was outrage at the Board's action. We received numerous calls and notes of support from the Tech community. If there had not been that kind of support, we would not have been successful at Virginia Tech, because one cannot fight for social justice when isolated and alone. It is the collective effort that fosters social change.

That collective, community effort began shortly after our arrival in Blacksburg in August 2002, when a group of concerned faculty met with us and told us that they wanted to help us in our struggle against the Board. This group wrote and circulated a petition that was forwarded to the Board of Visitors before their November 2002 meeting. A small number of folks also formed a group called Justice for Tech. This group initiated a nationwide letter-writing campaign on our behalf. In early spring 2003, Shelli was given copies of over 200 letters that had been sent to each member of the Board of Visitors, the Virginia Tech President, and the Governor of Virginia. There were letters from Tech alums, from colleagues we had never met from across the nation in our disciplines, from former students and colleagues who knew us personally, and from international supporters. In addition, the AAUP (American Association of University Professors), after reviewing the specifics of the case, wrote a letter to the Board and to the President of Virginia Tech condemning the Board's actions. Apparently, these letters were forwarded to the Board members as they came in, so that a steady stream of national and international attention was focused on the Board's perceived discriminatory actions throughout this time period. We have no doubt that the collective community activism that worked to put public pressure on the Board of Visitors–through the petition, the letters, the coverage in the *Chronicle of Higher Education,* a national lesbian magazine (see Rostow, 2003), and the protest by a group of faculty and student activists at the November 2002 Board of Visitors meeting–is the reason that a first step toward resolution occurred when a temporary position for Shelli was approved during the March 2003 Board meeting.

But at the same time that the Board of Visitors approved this temporary position, it took other actions that came as a surprise to almost everyone. Many viewed the March 2003 Board of Visitors' resolutions as a kind of "shock and awe" bombardment on a broad spectrum of diversity issues. Apparently, toward the end of the March 2003 Board meeting, the Rector convinced the other members of the Board that Tech's affirmative action policies were no longer necessary. In a move that preempted the Supreme Court, which had not yet decided upon the University of Michigan Affirmative Action case then before it, the Rector supposedly led the charge in convincing his fellow Board members that the best move for all concerned would be to eliminate Virginia Tech's affirmative action policies for hiring and admissions. A resolution was made to that effect, and it passed. Although equity issues were supposedly a concern behind the decision to remove affirmative action policy affecting admissions, policies regarding legacy admissions were not addressed (see Bartlett & Rooney, 2003).

And, if that wasn't enough for one meeting, the Board also decided to remove sexual orientation from Tech's non-discrimination policy. Specifically, at the same meeting in which a temporary, 12-month, re-

stricted, faculty research appointment for Shelli was approved by the
Board of Visitors, the Board also decided that discrimination on the basis of sexual orientation would no longer be covered in Tech's official
non-discrimination policy. This last gesture appeared to be, in our opin-
ion, a bit of a personal slap in the face and was just further confirmation
for us, and others, that sexual orientation had been and perhaps
continued to be an issue for some members of the Board.

But, again, there's a positive side to this chain of events. At Virginia
Tech, a campus that is not known for its social justice activism, the collective community response and coalition building that was prompted
by the Board's March 2003 actions was something we imagine that no
one on the Board predicted. It was empowering to be a part of and inspired by the students, staff, faculty, administrators, and community
members who worked together to try to convince the Board of Visitors
that their March 2003 decisions did not represent the values of the larger
university and Blacksburg communities. While unified coalitions of
different groups are fragile and often difficult to sustain, the spring of
2003 brought together a strong coalition of groups who took up one another's agendas within that historical moment. Social justice activism
around sexual orientation that doesn't recognize and engage other
marginalized identities, such as race, class, dis/ability, and so forth, is a
kind of "single-issue politics" that "is not only elusive but counterpro-
ductive" (Blasius, 2001, p. 12). It was an opportunity for the LGBT faculty, staff, and students to engage in anti-racism work and connect with
students of color who were fighting against the Board of Visitors' resolution that ended affirmative action, and it was an opportunity for students of color to do anti-homophobia work as well, as they fought
against the Board's removal of sexual orientation from the non-
discrimination statement.

Following a campus rally and involvement on the part of the local
and regional NAACP, a special meeting of the Board of Visitors was
called at the request of several Board members. April 6, 2003, marked
another historical and memorable event for Tech when the Board in a
public (and well-attended) meeting debated and then voted to rescind its
March 2003 resolutions. Affirmative action policies were reestablished
and sexual orientation was officially included in the Virginia Tech non-
discrimination policy.

One of the important victories for the LGBT students, faculty, staff,
and administrators at Virginia Tech was the reaffirmation of the very
broad non-discrimination policy. The inclusion of sexual orientation as
a protected category in the Virginia Tech non-discrimination policy has

a complex history. Like many institutions of higher education, Virginia Tech first began discussions of adding sexual orientation to its non-discrimination policy in the late 1980s. The initial push for inclusion of sexual orientation came from the student LGBT group on campus, which wanted Virginia Tech's non-discrimination policy to better reflect the welcoming and acceptance of lesbian, gay, bisexual, and transgender students and employees in light of Tech's diversity goals and its broad mission statement. A resolution adding sexual orientation to the non-discrimination policy was first discussed in Virginia Tech's University Council in 1990, and referred to the Equal Opportunity / Affirmative Action Committee for further consideration (Virginia Tech Governance Minutes Archive, 1990). Discussions about the policy also went on in the Faculty Senate, and a resolution was passed by the University Council in 1991 (Virginia Tech Governance Minutes Archive, 1991). Although the Board of Visitors apparently did not formally approve of the policy change, from 1991 to 2002 there seemed to have been little concern with the policy. Following the cancellation of Shelli's initial contract, however, some members of the Board supposedly believed that the inclusion of sexual orientation in the non-discrimination policy had never been approved by the Board and that the policy superceded non-discrimination guidelines of the state of Virginia and would likely not stand up to challenge in a court of law because of Dillon's Rule.[1]

Arguably, though, the 1991 version of the non-discrimination statement began to function as *de facto* policy in 1991 when the new, more inclusive non-discrimination policy was shortly thereafter added to all of Virginia Tech's employment and admissions materials, including the addition of the new policy to all of Tech's Websites regarding employment and admissions. Again, whether or not the policy was ever officially approved, the Board of Visitors recognized its *de facto* presence as a governing policy of Tech when, on March 10, 2003, they voted to remove sexual orientation from Tech's non-discrimination policy. After the student protests and the collective community activism helped stir the Board into the April 6, 2003, emergency session, however, the Board of Visitors reversed their March 10 resolution and voted to reinstate sexual orientation into the non-discrimination policy. Thus, the Board has now officially approved the language of Tech's current, very broadly inclusive non-discrimination policy (Board Meeting Minutes, 2003).

Institutions of higher education often espouse a rationale for diversity that is similar to the model that Corvin and Wiggins (1989) emphasize, which includes the theoretical premise that it is important to learn "about various cultural groups (i.e., cultural worldviews) so that there is some understanding of how an individual from a particular group may experience life" (p. 105). The inclusion of sexual orientation in definitions of diverse populations recognizes that life experiences for members of the LGBT community may well be different from the dominant cultural group in certain ways, and that a diverse community in an educational setting can work to help dispel the myths about diverse sexualities perpetuated by the heteronormativity of the dominant cultural values in the U.S. In other words, the theory that informs Tech's (and other educational institutions') non-discrimination practices recognizes the existence of homophobia that translates into discrimination, violence, prejudice, and the lack of civil rights protections in the larger society. Most colleges and universities recognize that homophobia should not govern the practices of institutions of higher education, since their articulated goals include efforts to create a diverse student, staff, and faculty population. Explicit gender and sexuality theories recognize the existence of a cultural heterosexism that works to exclude the needs, concerns, and life experiences of those who are not heterosexual (Blumenfeld 1992), and these theories directly and indirectly inform the addition of sexual orientation to the non-discrimination policies at colleges and universities.

The April 2003 inclusion of sexual orientation in Tech's non-discrimination policy indicates to the public and to peer institutions that Virginia Tech values diversity and welcomes members of the LGBT community into all aspects of the university. Change will not really be effective, however, unless our institutions of higher learning examine the ways they perpetuate traditional and exclusionary dominant cultural values, including heteronormativity, throughout all facets of the institution. A broader analysis of potential structural and curricular reforms should be undertaken, but such an analysis would only be useful if it undertook the process of critically engaging the underlying ideology of both policy and curricula. In other words, to truly examine and reform policy to reflect the institution's stated goals about fostering a diverse community, there should be a critical awareness of the rhetoric that merely suggests superficial diversity goals. Policies and curricula must be created that actually move beyond empty rhetoric and toward transformation of the institution, the community, and the broader society. As Louis Althusser (1969) argues in his classic essay on ideology and the state, educational systems (unless intent on exposing and critiquing the dominant ideology) function as an "ideological state apparatus," an agent of the state, and work to reproduce and maintain the hegemony of inequity and the unequal distribution of power (157). In order for higher education to actually foster social change, such critically engaged analyses will need to accompany and inform policy change.

VIRGINIA TECH–THE REST OF THE STORY

Even though the "three-steps back" events of the tumultuous academic year of 2002-2003 might initially indicate that Virginia Tech is not a forward-looking institution, interestingly enough, the events of 2002-2003 have actually helped propel Virginia Tech forward, accelerating its progress toward becoming a 21st-century university. Every year the regular rotation of Board members serving their allotted four-year terms allows the Governor of the Commonwealth of Virginia to appoint between three and four new members to the Board of Visitors. (The Governor may also choose to reappoint Board members, who may serve no more than two consecutive terms.) Presumably due in large part to the local, regional, and national activism surrounding the controversies at Virginia Tech, the Democratic Governor's appointments during this time period held more liberal and progressive views than the previous Republican appointees. At its November 3, 2003, meeting, the Board approved a permanent position for Shelli among its personnel actions. In addition to her administrative position in Learning Technologies, she was appointed Associate Professor with tenure in the Department of English (Bartlett, 2003). This was a major victory for the coalition at Virginia Tech. The results of the collective efforts and the ongoing fight for social justice would be visible in the Board's ratification of the permanent position for Shelli as well as in the articulation of its commitment to diversity during the 2004 academic year.

Democratic Governor Mark Warner's appointments have clearly changed the nature and the political leanings of the Board. The changes in membership allowed for the unexpected action the Board took in June 2004 when it replaced its sitting Rector, who still had one year remaining on his appointment, with a newly elected Rector (Minutes, 2004). With this change in leadership and membership, the 2004-2005 Board of Visitors has a renewed focus on diversity, especially by the members of the Academic Affairs Committee. Based upon the priorities established by the Provost and his leadership team, the Academic Affairs Committee has focused its work in three areas: faculty affairs, graduate education, and diversity.

The senior leadership of the university has also focused increased attention and priority to diversity and to the establishment of a welcoming environment for diverse faculty, staff and students. Most visible is the strengthened and public commitment to diversity by the Provost's Office and his leadership team. Examples include the development and implementation of dual-career hiring guidelines for hiring faculty, the re-energizing of the leadership role of the Vice President for Multicultural Affairs, and the activation of the Commission on Equal Opportunity and Diversity.

Dual-career couples are now once again on the radar screen for faculty hires, including same-sex domestic partners. Tech recently recruited and successfully hired a highly sought after female faculty member following newly drafted dual-career hiring guidelines. Seeing the same-sex couple and the departmental faculty (and wives) enjoying dinner at a local restaurant during the candidate's visit, it seemed so normative. It was hard to believe such a big change had occurred in just two years.

The awareness and inclusion of sexual orientation as part and parcel of diversity is now representative of Virginia Tech's efforts to become a top tier 21st-century university. The Vice President for Multicultural Affairs and the Commission on Equal Opportunity and Diversity took the lead in drafting a new university document entitled "The Virginia Tech Principles of Community," which includes LGBT individuals as a recognized component of the university community. There is also a new "Diversity Matters" document, which is a statement about the centrality of diversity to the university mission, and this year saw renewed vigor in organizing the annual Diversity Summit. Student activism, which helped to spark action in 2003, also continues. The D.R.O.P. Alliance, a multicultural student group whose acronym stands for Direct Resistance of Privilege, created the PATH Pledge (the Progressive Action Towards Humanity pledge) for this Diversity Summit–a call for individual and institutional accountability for continuing to change the climate around diversity issues.

On January 21, 2005, the 8th Annual Virginia Tech Diversity Summit was held. The Summit had the largest number of participants ever. In addition to the students, staff, and faculty in attendance, the President, the Provost and most members of the senior administration also participated. The new Rector of the Board of Visitors was an active participant and spoke at the end of the Summit, articulating a message that indicated a clear difference between the Board's leadership of 2002 and the Board's leadership in 2005. The Rector publicly reaffirmed his personal commitment to diversity and that of the Board of Visitors. He congratulated the university community on our progress toward a stronger commitment to diversity and social justice. And, he indicated his desire and pleasure to share "The Virginia Tech Principles of Community" with the rest of the Board members and his desire to sign the document at the March 2005 Board of Visitors meeting.

For those of us who were there at the beginning of this adventure in activism at Virginia Tech, the Rector's words held significance beyond the actual words he spoke. On some days, it has felt like a long and hard two and a half years since we first arrived at Virginia Tech in August 2002, and yet it is also true that the institution has changed in dramatic ways in a short two and a half years. The journey is not over. There is still much work to be done, but the direction is clear. And, again, perhaps the most important point is that we are not alone in this work here at Virginia Tech. In fact, our experiences at Virginia Tech make us reflect on the truth of the oft-quoted phrase, attributed to Margaret Mead: "Never doubt that a small group of committed citizens can change the world. Indeed, it's the only thing that ever has."

NOTE

1. Dillon's Rule was adopted by Virginia in the late 1800s and works to restrict the independence of local governments to make laws or ordinances that differ from state law. Interestingly, however, Dillon's Rule does not apparently apply to higher education, even though many administrators seem to believe it prohibits their ability to enforce policy that may be in conflict with state law. When the University of Virginia was exploring extending employee benefits to same-sex couples, those against the efforts cited the Dillon Rule in arguing that the University of Virginia would not be allowed to institute such a policy. "However, the legal tenet of Virginia law that mandates state agencies and municipalities not deviate from state guidelines (more commonly known as Dillon's Rule), specifically does not apply to colleges and universities. In this respect, the University has more authority to expand upon state guidelines than state agencies or municipalities" (Equality in granting benefits, 2003).

REFERENCES

Althusser, Louis. (1969, 1971). Ideology and ideological state apparatuses. *Lenin and Philosophy.* New York: Monthly Review Press.
Bartlett, T. (2002, November 22). Reversal of fortune: Virginia Tech rescinds an offer to a new dean's lesbian partner and ignites a controversy. *The Chronicle of Higher Education,* A12-14.

Bartlett, T. & Rooney M. (2003, March 28). Runaway board?: Unilateral actions at Virginia Tech raise questions about the proper role of trustees. *The Chronicle of Higher Education,* A25-26.

Bartlett, T. (2003, November 21). After the fact: Virginia Tech makes good on a hiring offer. *The Chronicle of Higher Education,* A8.

Blasius, M. (2001). Introduction. *Sexual Identities, Queer Politics,* ed., M. Blasius. Princeton: Princeton University Press, 3-19.

Blumenfeld, W. J. (Ed.) 1992. *Homophobia: How we all pay the price.* Boston: Beacon Press.

Board Meeting Minutes. (2003, April 6). Resolution rescinding the "resolution . . . articulating the university's policy against discrimination." Retrieved 1-22-05, from *http://www.bov.vt.edu/03-04-06minutes/03-04-06minutes.html*

Corvin, S. A. & Wiggins, F. (1989). An antiracism training model for white professionals. *Journal of Multicultural Counseling and Development, 17,* 104-114.

Employment Non-discrimination Act. Retrieved 1-16-05, from *http://www.hrc.org/Template.cfm?Section=Employment_Non-Discrimination_Act*

Equality in granting benefits. (2003, August 28). *Cavalier Daily,* Retrieved, 1-16-05, from *http://www.cavalierdaily.com/CVArticle.asp?ID=16390&pid=1029*

Gaard, Greta. (1996). Anti-lesbian intellectual harassment in the academy. In *Antifeminism in the Academy,* eds. V. Clark, S.N. Garner, M. Higonnet, and K.H. Katrak. New York: Routledge, 115-140.

Minutes. (2002, June 3). Salary and personnel actions closed session items. Virginia Tech Board of Visitors, President's Office, Virginia Tech, 1-9.

Minutes. (2004, June 7). Report of the nominating committee, 15-16. Retrieved, 1-22-05, from *http://www.bov.vt.edu/04-06-07minutes/04-06-07Minutes.pdf*

Report of the Academic Affairs Committee. (2002, June 3). Virginia Tech Board of Visitors. President's Office, Virginia Tech, 1-2.

Rich, A. (1983). Compulsory heterosexuality and lesbian existence. In *Powers of desire: The politics of sexuality,* eds. A. Snitow, C. Stansell, and S. Thompson, 177-206. New York: Monthly Review Press.

Rostow, A. (2003, April). Place of hire learning: A Virginia college town rallies around a lesbian teacher whose contract was suspiciously nullified. *Girlfriends,* 12-13.

Steward, D. (2003). Working toward equality. *Academe,* July-August 2003, 29-33.

Virginia Tech Governance Minutes Archive. (1990, December 3). University Council Minutes, Retrieved on 1-12-05, from *http://spec.lib.vt.edu/minutes/ucm/1990/December+3++1990.html*

Virginia Tech Governance Minutes Archive. (1991, February 4). University Council Minutes, Retrieved on 1-12-05, from *http://spec.lib.vt.edu/minutes/ucm/1991/February+4++1991.html*

Unruly Democracy and the Privileges of Public Intimacy: (Same) Sex Spousal Hiring in Academia

Chantal Nadeau

Concordia University, Montreal

SUMMARY. Within the context of a discussion of lesbian academic couples there is something to be said about the (dis)pleasures and profits of a heteronormative practice such as spousal hiring and how much this privilege reveals the broader systemic discrimination vis-à-vis sexual and gender claims in our academic institutions. Two issues emerge from its (questionable) application: (1) How a privilege such as spousal hiring intersects with institutional policies concerning sexual diversity; and in light of this,

Chantal Nadeau is Associate Professor of Communication Studies at Concordia University (Montréal) where she teaches queer theory, postcolonial studies and media criticism. Her first book *Fur Nation: From the Beaver to Brigitte Bardot* (Routledge, 2001) offers a re-mapping of Canadian history by reclaiming the centrality of beaver(s) in the sexualization of the nation. Her current research addresses the intersections between queers, rights and democracy. She is working on her second book, entitled *Beastly Politics: Queers, Rights and Democracy* (working title).

Author note: This article is a reworked and expanded version of my earlier argument on spouse hirings; see Chantal Nadeau, "Unruly Privileges, or La Loi Du Silence: Same-Sex Spousal Hiring in Academia," 3 Oct.1999, CULSTUD-L. Available: *http://www.cas.usf.edu/communication/rodman/cultstud/columns.html*.

[Haworth co-indexing entry note]: "Unruly Democracy and the Privileges of Public Intimacy: (Same) Sex Spousal Hiring in Academia." Nadeau, Chantal. Co-published simultaneously in *Journal of Lesbian Studies* (Harrington Park Press, an imprint of The Haworth Press, Inc.) Vol. 9, No. 4, 2005, pp. 89-105; and: *Lesbian Academic Couples* (ed: Michelle Gibson, and Deborah T. Meem) Harrington Park Press, an imprint of The Haworth Press, Inc., 2005, pp. 89-105. Single or multiple copies of this article are available for a fee from The Haworth Document Delivery Service [1-800-HAWORTH, 9:00 a.m. - 5:00 p.m. (EST). E-mail address: docdelivery@haworthpress.com].

(2) Why queer or lesbian couples shouldn't embrace dubious spousal hiring incentives. *[Article copies available for a fee from The Haworth Document Delivery Service: 1-800-HAWORTH. E-mail address: <docdelivery@haworthpress.com> Website: <http://www.HaworthPress.com> © 2005 by The Haworth Press, Inc. All rights reserved.]*

KEYWORDS. Lesbian, academic couple, spousal hiring, domestic partner benefits, queer

One is too few, and two is only one possibility.

–Donna Haraway, *Cyborg Manifesto*

While the current race for the recognition of gay and lesbian rights in Western democracies seems to have largely been dominated by same-sex marital and domestic arrangement claims, there remain domains of contention where the romantic bonds between same-sex partners have not yet attracted the public eye. One can reflect, for example, on the issue of same-sex partner hiring in academia. Whether it pertains to such an infinitesimal portion of its population or it is perceived as less a matter of rights than of a recognition of intimate bonds that intersect with intellectual capital, the social and economic costs of spousal hiring–especially same-sex spousal hiring–are yet to be fully considered and weighed.[1] Within the context of this discussion of Lesbian Academic Couples there is something to be said about the (dis)pleasures and profits of a heteronormative practice such as spousal hiring and how much this little privilege reveals the broader systemic discrimination vis-à-vis sexual and gender claims in our academic institutions. Although this essay doesn't pretend to uncover all the dirty little secrets surrounding this very (un)official practice (if it did, there would be enough material for a three-part exclusive cover story in *Harper's*), my paper aims at reflecting upon two issues that emerge from its (questionable) application:

1. How a privilege such as spousal hiring intersects with institutional policies concerning sexual diversity; and in light of this,
2. Why queer or lesbian couples shouldn't embrace dubious spousal hiring incentives.

My feelings towards this contradictory issue are mixed to say the least and troubled by a nexus of ideological, political and economic views on how both "coupledom" and sexuality–in their heteronormative and homonormative beauty–operate outside and inside the academic machine. To make things murkier, academics, let's be honest, occupy a privileged position in the labor structure of the society and enjoy a panoply of "benefits" and other corporate privileges that are not accessible to the majority of workers. So much for my Marxist sensitivity and class analysis of academic culture and intellectual capital mobility. Nevertheless, I strongly believe that when academic culture rhymes with sexual identity, discriminatory practices towards gay and lesbian academic couples as well as queer individuals are rampant and definitely part of the medley of unruly privileges that make the brain business work. Because "privileges" these days stand as the *modus operandi* for a conception of equality that is foremost understood in terms of value (Aristotle), it emerges as a site of segregation for gays and lesbians. For every gay and lesbian couple who makes it to the Dean's Office, how many straight couples have the privilege of being shooed in, behind closed doors, and without having to be singled out as the queer next door?

I am using here the expression "unruly privileges"–in lieu of rights or benefits–in order to offer a critical reflection on the ways that benefits and privileges are too often confused (wrongly) with rights. In particular, I evoke the academic culture surrounding spousal hiring to reflect critically on the tendency to bring under one umbrella sexuality and so-called rights as a matter of measuring the level of inclusion or exclusion members of certain communities fall under–a tendency that unfortunately short-circuits any attempt to question the assumptions behind the LGBT community's efforts to achieve equality at any cost: visibility and inclusion = progress and recognition. The term *unruly* refers on one hand to defiant, unrestrained, anarchic and ungovernable (Roget's), and on the other to a lack of control and discipline over certain behaviors or targeted groups (OED). I wish to suggest here that the politics and economy of spousal hiring in academia encompasses both paradoxical practices. Spousal hiring is intrinsically part of a discriminatory system whose subjects are likely to be seen as either "sexual public vectors" or as sexually docile, i.e., unnoticed. If academic institutions have taken the initiative to incorporate spousal hiring into their hiring practices or head-hunting priorities without creating official policies, it is because it is definitely queer (in its etymological sense of odd, weird) for institutions to be complicit with the sexual intimacies of their members since everything in an academic institution is about the close monitoring of sexual exposure and the so-called ethics of sex.

In this line, this "practice" unpacks in a revealing way how sexuality, gender and entitlement deeply inform the modalities of control and discipline of certain groups over others in academia. My argument is structured by two observations. On one hand, I question how a practice that is, like it or not, defined by sexual motif escapes the systemic policing of sexual conduct in the institution. On the other hand, I demonstrate that spousal hiring sabotages attempts at establishing more democratic strategies for queer inclusion and ultimately plays against queers. The various intertwined discourses of inclusiveness, family welfare, and academic performance that are evoked to legitimate spousal hiring are then even more telling: because the unruly privilege at stake here is indeed a heteronormative one; in a strange reversal of fortune, it is the very heteronormative texture of spousal hiring privilege that makes it unruly, and henceforth outside the law of equity.

MARRIED WITH(IN) ACADEMIA

Why should a university administration take on managing, if not solving, the logistics of domestic mobility? Of interest here is the rational line "universities have to." My response is, why do they?

In order to make my claim, instead of taking the expected and "natural" position of advocating for all queer couples the same privilege extended to heterosexual academic couples regarding "compassionate" spousal hiring, I wish to offer a critical reflection on the issues that emerge from this unruly privilege. My position seeks to uncover the consequences of enforcing a potential practice that, far from leading to "inclusion" or recognition of lesbian couples in academia, on the contrary perpetuates an arbitrary structure of feelings that has very little to contribute to the actual debate on equal/equivalent rights for all members of a community, sexual divide aside. In other words, spousal hiring beyond sexual identity-based screening has never been and will never be about rights: on the contrary, it feeds a heteronormative structure of labor that sets the explicit terms under which (or what and whose) gender, race and sexuality are likely either to be profitable or damaging to the institution. Forgive me for not being a champion for same-sex spousal hiring as I believe that spousal hiring is part of the same rhetoric and the same system of discriminatory practices and policies that aim at monitoring and keeping at bay certain types of sexual behaviors while welcoming (in the most hypocritical way) sexual and gender diversity on the surface. What spousal hirings expose is the fact that value and status in academia are still the perquisites of a few privileged members, and that this select club is rarely a lesbian hub, coupled or not.

What is fascinating in these circumstances is the fact that most administrative units demonstrate absolutely no desire to commit towards their gay and lesbian members beyond the usual affirmative action policy. Indeed, a growing number of universities and colleges are now granting same-sex partner benefits, including my home institution in Montréal, Concordia University.[2] This is worth mentioning in these days where most gay and lesbian discourses measure success in terms of visibility, tax credits, and other monetary benefits that might add up to some sort of mathematical formula for equality and good citizenry. However, this kaleidoscopic model of quantified equality carries at its core its poisonous trade-off: only what is out there and measurable can be counted as positive inclusion. To put it bluntly: same-sex benefits provisions impinge on a policy that is easily applicable under very precise rules, while spousal hiring falls in the category of the unruly privilege. One is about the liberal and romantic view of access to wealth as the paragon of equality: the other feeds a strict economy of inclusion/exclusion that responds to obscure considerations of who has value (and brain capital) on the academic market, so "they" say, all things considered. The latter rhetoric could easily be that of the official discourse on an unruly privilege.

My reading is slightly different: I argue that spousal hiring as a selected practice in academia turns literally political issues (the contentious aspect of spouse as sexual provision) into moralistic ones (family matters). Exit sexuality and heteronormativity, welcome family reunion and double hiring as a time and money saver.[3] This is the unruly privilege of being heteronormatively positioned, a quality that, alas, extends to homosexual conformism, a phenomenon termed by some scholars "homonormativity" (Warner 1999, Duggan 2003, 2004).[4]

But my question is the following: what happens if we repudiate and expel the moralistic rationale and reestablish the politics of sex (and gender) at the center of a critical analysis of the business of spousal hiring?[5] This is even more problematic if we factor in that spousal hiring might be about sexuality and intimacy, a domain that is usually carefully monitored by the academic culture. Most institutions have policies regarding the monitoring of acceptable and unacceptable sexual conduct within their walls, either in terms of sexual harassment or the screening of sexual conduct between faculty and students (including the blurred domain of consensual relations that is dismissed even more because it is framed as conflict of interests).[6] We might argue that all the above examples have to do with sex, and that spousal hiring is not about sex. But if the label "spouse" is asexual, what are spouses about, hmmm? Caring?

Spousal hiring is a hidden rule because it allows one to make invisible what normally should be exposed to the same monitoring that usually affects other tropes of sexuality in academia. In other words, spousal hiring is about the sexuality that should dare to be exposed as such. The reason that same-sex spousal hiring is so marginal is that it incidentally discloses in the most ready fashion what spouses are: a sexualized duo, a reality that is downplayed in spousal hirings involving heterosexual partners, while other considerations such as family rights are more likely to be put forward to justify such practice.[7] Yet what happens when what is at stake is a matter of privilege? Same-sex spousal hiring en masse would suddenly force academia to move spousal hiring from a privileged status to the level of what constitutes a sexual policy, which would mean a public exposure of a thus far quite secretive process.

THE STATE OF THE AFFAIR: A QUEER LOOK

In most cases, the privilege of heterosexual spousal hiring in academia is, if not unspoken, then a soft spoken practice at best, and its applications vary from one institution to another. While some universities or colleges have decided to move forward and develop built-in recommendations regarding spousal hiring (for tenured or limited-term hirings), most of these institutions have deliberately chosen to elide the gender and queer factor from spousal hiring, even though many of them recognize same-sex partners in their benefits packages. The silence here is not fortuitous; on the contrary, it speaks to the ways that the term "spouse" is still very much culturally defined along the line of family life, "marriage," or any other form of heteronormative intimacy that is constructed as a pillar of stability and security. The fact that a growing number of provincial, state and federal laws extend the definition of spouses to same-sex partners does not impinge on the way that spousal hiring is understood. Again, the fact that spousal hiring is not a policy in most cases but only a recruitment and retention bargaining chip is what allows discrimination to settle in and function at its best. As an enticing value, it escapes the sexual/equity eye, yet it does contribute to the creation within the walls of academe a double-standard system of sex, to echo Gayle Rubin,[8] within which sexuality is the unspoken bait and gender is still imagined as binary.

The question becomes then: do institutions have official policies or "guidelines" regarding spousal hiring, or is the practice only legendary? For the purpose of my argument, I decided to look randomly and certainly not thoroughly at some local examples (my "investigation" is limited to Canada), and indeed I found traces of spousal hiring mentioned. It came as no surprise that administrators would bring the topic to the table in a country so competitively exposed to the American market; the retention factor is often brought forward by academic institutions to limit brain mobility, i.e., what has come to be known as *l'exode des cerveaux* [Editors' note: in colloquial English, brain drain].

A quick analysis of the situation in this country speaks volumes. First observation: There are significant differences among institutions regarding the official and non-official implementation of the economy of spousal hiring. While some institutions do indeed have a spousal hiring policy (University of Calgary, Queen's, University),[9] most of them officially choose to present themselves as a welcoming resource to help spouses find employment within or outside academia. In some cases, employment equity initiatives act as a liaison, yet sexual orientation is scarcely mentioned in the definition of spouses. True, anti-discrimination and equity policies forbid search committees or administrators from asking potential candidates about their sexual orientation during interviews. Yet what is telling here is when not specified, most of these policies or guidelines assume that "spouses" indeed means spouses of opposite sex. Moreover, it would be interesting to know who is the spousal hiring target in most cases: Is it a woman? Or a man? What deal has she/he been offered? The usual adjunct position, a gendered ghetto in so many instances? A limited appointment? A tenured one? On the other hand, when once in a while an individual success story (namely a story that involves two same-sex spouses) emerges from the darkness and breaks the news in high-profile academic media (say the *Chronicle of Higher Education*), one can't help but ask: Which kind of logic of equality is displayed and produced here? For the benefit of whom? And why does sexual identity suddenly matter? Or maybe it doesn't. It is no coincidence that sexual orientation or *sexe tout court* is always mentioned in regard to equity or discrimination, whereas spousal hiring is tied to "quality of life."[10]

If it is true that spousal hiring aims at fulfilling expectations regarding "quality of life" (no word here about "romantic love" or *fucking*), it is clear that spousal hiring speaks directly to marriage politics and the traditional hierarchy between singles and couples in society. One would think that thirty years of feminism would have led to more liberal social assumptions, yet looking at the roaring movement over same-sex unions and marriages across Western democracies, one is right to be puzzled by the ways couples and spouses have become "the" ultimate symbol of recognition for lesbians and gays in our society. In the maze of discourses about rights and other claims regarding the equation "sexual identity" and "fair distribution of wealth," a rather scarce space is allocated to a discussion of the system of compulsory coupledom as the epitome of stability and commitment vis-à-vis civic institutions, including our venerable universities. Or maybe universities are as mercantile as the private sector when it comes down to the maximization of the workforce. We could argue that as studies show that women and men in couples are likely to live longer,[11] spousal hiring constitutes, all things considered, a better investment for an employer. No matter what objection one could raise, academic administrators and the general population alike are going for who fits into the box of "family." In this rhetoric of optimization of labor forces, allow me to raise some serious concerns about which couples' lives are actually under scrutiny. My hunch is that the couple is the straight one. If we push the equality by calculus argument to its end, we rightly wonder why universities don't hire more lesbian academic couples, since women in most industrial countries have a longer life expectancy than men. Or maybe this is it: women live longer, requiring more pension payout, and then the hiring of lesbian academic couples again becomes a matter of one is okay, two cost too much.

Because the gender factor is not uniformly welcome as part of the spousal hiring game, it is important to understand and to situate such an unruly practice in a context of sexual discrimination, not only toward gay and lesbian academic couples, but also toward gay and lesbian faculty who are by default always constituted as "single," with all the pressure that brings regarding the organization of labor and distribution of tasks within the university. Actually, a lot needs to be said and analyzed–and I'm afraid that I'm limited by space here from developing this point, and that so far I have only hinted at it–about the relationship between sexuality and labor in the production of academic intellectual life.

I have already highlighted how spousal hiring is a very nebulous condition, or privilege, neither easily circumscribed, nor clearly stated, and most of the time a secret weapon used at the "discretion" of the hiring committee, or the Faculty. However, what is interesting in most of the rhetorics at work in the sexual divide discussed above is that the sheer nebulousness of privilege attached to spousal hiring just makes it easier to discard the fact that what is an unruly although possible practice for heterosexuals becomes an obscure impossibility for gay and lesbian couples. This becomes even more explicit if you take the practice of spousal hiring for candidates for a teaching position. Spousal hiring doesn't occur through specified rules of hiring, but rather through a set of official and unofficial channels within which the spouse of the newly hired or the "top candidate" would be considered for hiring in the same institution–given ideally that the partner is fully qualified, or even on some occasions, tenurable. For heterosexual couples, from the very outset of the hiring process, way before the hiring becomes a reality, spousal hiring is an assumed part of the process, even implicit in the process of serenading future candidates. It is implicit in and actually part of the hiring package of the candidate selected, whether s/he is an academic star or not. For gay and lesbian couples, things are far from being so. From the very beginning, the question of spousal hiring is silenced and completely erased from the process of the job search. I insist here: the exclusion is not a matter of visibility, but a question of institutional practices of silence around certain forms of intimacies over others. (I will address later what the growing movement for same-sex marriage might mean for queer academics and especially lesbians, since the recent polls show that lesbians have been the major consumers of marriage.)

Worse: the erasure of same sex couples in academia is not only a matter of institutional policy, but is equally "nourished" by other professors. While future colleagues might inquire about the eventuality of a long distance relationship for same-sex academic partners, these conversations are likely to be carried on behind closed doors, over cocktails, in a benign and supportive fashion, but nonetheless safely remote from the public eye of the official hiring process. This issue is troubled by the fact that most gays and lesbians involved in such situations keep silent on such matters. The legitimacy of the hiring committee's silence on spousal hiring is further reinforced by most candidates' fear of calling attention to it. The rationale here is that our jobs are so hard to get anyway, what candidate would jeopardize her chances by even bringing up such an issue? To bring up the issue is to break the silence around the politics of heterosexual spousal hiring privileges. In such a context and as far as gay and lesbian rights are concerned, the rule that prevails is overruled by the privilege granted automatically to most heterosexual candidates involved in such a process.

What I wish to convey here is that, while history, gossip, and department faculty lists all over the continent have shown us that "spousal sumptuary hiring laws" seem to have prevailed for heterosexual couples, the same is far from being true for gay and lesbian partners. In the few exceptions where a same-sex partner has actually been welcomed to an institution along with the new hire, those few marginal cases are used as an alibi, a way to exhibit the token successful queer as evidence of institutional commitment, at once making blurry the unspoken discarded cases. This is not to say that heterosexual academic couples aren't facing any issues in terms of hiring; but whereas heterosexual academics are considered as couples, queers are necessarily framed as singles. It is not only a question of discrimination, but also the rule of denial, silencing, and rejection of gay and lesbian identity and culture, under a very strict politics of compulsory heterosexual privilege. What is at stake here is not only a culture of difference and ways of representing and speaking for different subjects, but also a politics of difference strictly monitored for the sake of maintaining a safe heterosexual visibility.

This question of "rights" vs. privilege is what has actually been framed as central in the most recent debates around gay and lesbian equity, visibility, coming out. There is something in these debates that troubles me profoundly, because most of the debates obscure the complexities that emerge from "framing rights" as the main emancipatory way for the gay and lesbian minority to reach equality and gain the same privileges as the heterosexual majority. I do not pretend to be an expert on questions of discrimination and rights. However, what I certainly can address is how issues of visibility and practices of regulation of sexual differences within universities and colleges are not separated from the same rhetoric of competition that too often monopolizes claims for gay and lesbian rights that tend to separate the good queers from the bad ones. Such an attitude towards a meritorious equity outside and inside the academic machine is not only ruled by sexual politics, but is completely mapped by segregated sexual assumptions about intellectual/pedagogical practices and (mis)behaviors.

THE ECONOMY OF THE INVISIBLE

As it is a privilege, spousal hiring falls in the category of the economy of the invisible, which doesn't mean that it is economically invisible. Hundreds of years of racism and sexism have allowed a system of class

and caste to survive economically on the basis of this exploitative structure. In other words, as a privilege, spousal hiring can't be visible, but
its consequences are necessarily economically and monetarily visible.
So is marriage. Within traditional marital boundaries, because it is in
principle invisible rather than ruled, heterosexuality also becomes invisible, erasing the fact that spousal hiring is commanded by sexual politics. Paradoxically, what becomes visible though, even too visible, is
same-sex relationships. Herein lies the urge not to address it in the process of hiring a queer candidate, because it goes against the logic and the
rationale of the privilege.

I have hinted earlier at the question of whether same-sex marriage
might change the ways spousal hirings affect queer academic couples in
the near future. The question is of special interest in this publication on
lesbian academics as recent polls show that lesbians have been the
front-runners in seeking marriages and civil unions at city hall, where
the law allows, and that in a 3 to 1 proportion over gay men.[12] I am not
attempting to battle over the paradoxes of visibility and invisibility for
gays and lesbians. All things considered, the question seems obsolete.
However, what strikes me here is how the rights-based strategy of many
gay and lesbian groups obscures the incredible resources that society
possesses to go around the compulsory equality stated by the Charter of
Rights or any kind of other official document or social contract that con-
trols, regulates and monitors the space of equality for the citizen. What
we call privilege in economic terms refers bluntly to discriminatory
practice in social and political terms. Moreover, privileges and benefits
cost money and academia in this age of corporate architecture, course
sponsorship, and private endowments is more than ever about money.
Hence the systematic practice of limiting privileges to a so-called
demographically safe and stable population (queer lifestyle being
portrayed as unstable and highly risky).

This is why expanding privileges to more individuals won't solve the
problems that most academic institutions have with gay and lesbian
couples, i.e., that queer necessarily means duplication, no matter how
different the intellectual and pedagogical projects of the two partners
are. While two 19th century experts, three cultural studies scholars, four
Hollywood "thinkers" won't ever be seen as the same, and on the contrary will be evaluated in their fruitful complementarity, two lesbians
are already doomed to be too many. In other words, one of the core institutional problems with "queer," and even more with gendered queers, is
that whereas one might be seen as cute, even an asset, two are already
too much and represented in an exponential way. Or, to put it bluntly: a

lesbian scholar might be a promotional investment, but a lesbian academic couple is redundant and can only "ghettoize" knowledge. While straight spousal hirings are seen as a source of continuity, balance, and strong commitment towards the institution (i.e., an investment to the quality of life), same-sex spousal hirings are perceived as a dramatic (read excessive) representation of sexual politics in the institution, regardless of the areas of expertise or research pursued by the candidates. A queer academic couple–even not in the same department or the same faculty– threatens to unbalance the line of power that commands most academic units–which for anyone involved in the academic world constitutes a fraudulent reason, as other forms of alliances are likely to be equally, if not more, powerful than the fleshly ones.

Beyond internally regimented institutional policies, what is at stake here is the unruled and invisible privilege of keeping the space of knowledge and collegiality as heterosexual as it can be. This is why any intervention on behalf of truth and justice for the individual is necessarily exposed to the same law of silence, as well as the markets of rights and identities: temporary gratification obtained at the cost of deeper silences, and yes, "discriminatory" practices. This is why spousal hiring in its current form is not the ticket to more inclusiveness, visibility, recognition, etc.: it is a club with Masonic rules within which the neoliberal values of sexualized corporate individualism guide most of the decisions, including the segregated structures of governance over and recognition of what is or is not considered publicly sexual. Then the question remains: why should we as lesbian academics want so badly to be invited to this specific segregationist club? If there is a battle that lesbian academic couples should undertake, and I am saying this at the risk of sounding completely idealistic, it is to expose fiercely and mercilessly the hypocritical ways that academia deals with sexuality, because as with gender that is always about women, sexuality is always about queers. Period. As long as our institutions continue to compartmentalize sexuality according to hazardous rules of inclusion and exclusion with a questionable prejudice for coupling brains, I refuse to be part of this masquerade of "quality of life."

What is the alternative? If one would have to choose the least of all evils, one way to thwart this unruly privilege would be to make spousal hiring a provision under the rules and regulations of sexual conduct in academia. While the dominant practice now is to make it an exception, a favor granted to a few, a gesture not monitored or screened by any governance but the Dean's Office, to make it a provision will make spousal hiring into a question of ethics and responsibility shared by both the institution and the individuals involved. While advocating for more policing by the institution on sexual matters might be perceived as a political aberration for many gays and lesbians, I would like to reiterate here, on the contrary, that this time the spotlight won't be solely on queer (mis)behaviors, but also on straight behaviors. The goal then is to move spousal hiring, a dominant heterosexual privilege, from behind closed doors to a more public space where issues of fairness and equity prevail. For lesbian or other queer couples, such a solution might be a risky and costly one: among others, the obvious disclosure of intimacy and exposure to more homophobic reactions with dramatic consequences, including, as has happened before, an unsuccessful double hiring. Yet, it seems to me that this is a valid way to *limit*–and not erase–the scope within which sexuality is applied differently between queers and straights by academic culture. My comment here is motivated by the strong belief that spousal hiring is not likely to disappear; hence the urgency to make it a matter of public policy rather than a secret society ritual.

This is the prime of my argument: spousal hiring is informed by an economy of the invisible. This invisibility is a lucrative one, not only in terms of an exchange market, but also as a social and political constituency. In this sense, individual privileges aren't so much privileges as important elements of control and of instrumentalization of the economy of sexual identities. This is not a phenomenon that occurs exceptionally, but on a systematic basis. The apparent marginality of the issue of academic spousal hiring, superfluous, "micro-located" and exceptional as it may seem, shouldn't banalize the systematic regulation that afflicts lesbian, gay and queer sexuality within various societal institutions, from the legal apparatus, to the media, to the sanitized forum of academia. Lesbians as subjects to double discrimination (gender and sexuality) should know better that *one is too few . . . and two only one possibility.*

NOTES

1. Though not directly linked to my argument, I wish to mention some references pertinent to the contextualization of the relationships between lesbians and academic institutions: Doris Davenport, "Still Here: Ten Years Later . . . ," *Tilting the Tower*, ed. Linda Garber (New York & London: Routledge, 1999) and Mary Klages, "The Ins and Outs of a Lesbian Academic," *Tilting the Tower*, ed. Linda Garber (New York & London: Routledge, 1999). Also, for questions and issues related more specifically to the pedagogical and social contribution of academic lesbian/gay/queer studies, see the an-

thology *Inside Academia and Out: Lesbian/Gay/Queer Studies and Social Action*, Janice L. Ristock and Catherine G. Taylor, eds. (Toronto: University of Toronto Press, 1998).

2. For an overview of spousal hiring in the US, see Amy Benson Brown. "Keeping Company, Staying Power, Keeping Power." *The Academic Exchange* Oct./Nov. 2002, 3 July 2004. <http://www.emory.edu/ACAD_EXCHANGE/2002/sept/keepingsidebar. html>. Brown explains that "A survey of 360 institutions recently published in the *Journal of Higher Education* reports that 45 percent of research universities [note: i.e., in 2002] have spousal hiring policies, while only 20 percent of liberal arts colleges do. Accommodating spouses of new hires is standard practice at Michigan State University, for instance. And the provost of the University of Michigan contributes up to a third of the salary for a spousal hire." Then Brown brings in the gender issue of spousal hiring by noting that "Although spousal appointments remain controversial, the scent of stigma that sometimes lingered around the 'trailing spouse' is dissipating, as women sometimes are the most sought-after member of the pair."

3. For a typical example of celebratory representation of heterosexual couples in academia, see the following articles by Robin Wilson: "When Officemates Are Also Roommates," *The Chronicle of Higher Education* (1998); and for a follow-the-couple story that personalizes the spousal hiring issue: "A Couple's Struggle to Find Good Jobs in the Same City: He's at Yale; She's at Missouri; and the Humanities Job Market Makes Their Search a Challenge." *Chronicle of Higher Education* April 2000, 21 May 2004. <http://chronicle.com/free/v46/i33/33a00101.htm>.

4. See Michael Warner, *The Trouble with Normal: Sex Politics, and the the Ethics of Queer Life* (Cambridge, Massachusetts: Harvard University Press, 2000). Lisa Duggan discusses at length the tension of a new homonormativity guided by heteronormative boundaries in "The New Homonormativity: The Sexual Politics of Neoliberalism," *Materializing Democracy: Toward a Revitalized Cultural Politics*, ed. Russ Castronovo and Dana D. Nelson (Durham: Duke University Press, 2002), and in *The Twilight of Equality: Neoliberalism, Cultural Politics, and the Attack on Democracy* (Boston: Beacon Press, 2003).

5. Interestingly enough, a 25-page document prepared to evaluate strategies for equity at the University of Victoria in Canada mentions how spousal hiring policy is necessary to help create equity for women. See *University of Victoria Federal Contractors Program Compliance Review Report 1993-2003*, 2003, University of Victoria. Available: *http://web.uvic.ca/equity/FCP2003/Part1.pdf*.

6. For a discussion contrasting "consensual sex" vs. inclusions within sexual harassment policies in academia, see Jane Gallop, "Resisting Reasonableness," *Anecdotal Theory* (Durham: Duke University Press, 2002). Weaving her own experience with that of the story of a lesbian academic couple, one being a professor, the other her graduate student whose romance stirred the ire of the university board, Gallop offers an interesting angle on the issue, notably denouncing the random way institutions treat questions of sex in academia, notably when it comes to drawing the line between consensual sex and abuse of power. Gallop observes that "current academic relations policies are in fact more hospitable to casual sex that to serious romance." While "Campuses continue to treat consensual relations within their harassment policies" (68), they also find it unreasonable and unacceptable that a relationship might develop between a student and professor. Even though I don't necessarily subscribe to Gallop's position regarding her celebration of teaching as romance v. sex, a topic that was in fact the core of her book *Feminist Accused of Sexual Harrassment* (Durham: Duke Univer-

sity Press, 1997), I must say that her denunciation of the ways that consentual flings are less threatening than relationships before the eyes of Boards of Governors–and especially in the example of the two lesbians–speaks strongly to my way of conceptualizing how spousal hiring is constructed along the sexual identity divide.

7. For instance, the collective agreement at Université du Québec à Montréal (UQAM) that identifies "spouse" as same or opposite sex, while only opposite sex couples are included under children clauses. See the collective agreement between UQAM and its employees at: *Convention Collective Intervenue Entre L'uqam Et Le Seuqam*, 2002, UQAM. Available: *http://www.rhu.uqam.ca/relationspro/Documents/Convention Seuqam.pdf*. 19 May 2004.

8. Gayle Rubin, "Thinking Sex: Notes for a Radical Theory of the Politics of Sexuality," *The Lesbian and Gay Studies Reader*, eds. Henry Abelove, Michèle Aina Barale and David M. Halperin (New York: Routledge, 1993).

9. University of Calgary has a spousal hiring policy for members of a marriage or domestic partnership. It does not, however, specify if the policy applies to heterosexual or same-sex partnership. On the other hand, Queen's University's spousal hiring policy ratified in 2002 includes both same-sex and opposite sex unions. For a detailed description of the policy at Queen's, see the two following documents: 2002, QUFA Bargaining Committee Queen's University. Available: *http://www.queensu.ca/qufa/ Negotiations_Archives/Negotiations_2001-02/Settlement_2002-05.htm*, 20 May 2004, *Collective Agreement between Queen's University Faculty Association and Queen's University at Kingston*, 2002, Queen's University, Available: *http://www.queensu.ca/ qufa/Collective_Agreement/candx.htm*, 21 May 2004.

10. This is an argument made by Ruth Rees in an article on equity in academic hiring; see Ruth Rees. "Equity in Faculty Recruitment." *International Electronic Journal For Leadership in Learning* 28 Sept. 2000, 19 May 2004. <http://www.acs.ucalgary. ca/~iejll/volume4/rees_v4n12.html>.

11. See, for instance, how life insurance companies evaluate life expectancy. In a typical questionnaire example aiming at establishing the client profile, the rubric "Live with a spouse or a friend" hits +5 on the life expectancy chart as the "Live alone" gets−3. The questionnaire is reproduced in Shino Nemoto and Toren Finkel, "Ageing and the Mystery at Earles," *Nature: an international weekly journal of science* 429 (2004). Ironically, the "evidence" reappears in E. J. Graff's social history of marriage, *What Is Marriage For? The Strange Social History of Our Most Intimate Institution* (Boston: Beacon Press). While discussing the case for same-sex marriage from an economic point of view, the lesbian activist and journalist asserts that ". . . Married people live longer, healthier, more productive lives (. . .). Whether measuring by death rate, morbidity (health problems such as diabetes, kidney disease, or ischemic heart disease), subjective or stress-related complaints (dizziness, shortness of breath, achiness, days in bed during past year, asthma, headaches), or psychiatric problems (clinical depression or debilitating anxiety after a cancer diagnosis), married people do better than unmarried–single, widowed, divorced" (2004, 44-45). Although Graff based her argument on recent statistical research, her conclusions reiterate one of the oldest statistical research reports on health and marriage: William Farr's "Marriage is a Healthy State," published in 1858, a survey that Graff quotes at length.

12. This "fact" is mostly established in the US context and is reported by Michael Bronski in *The Nation* forum on marriage, Michael Bronski. "Can Marriage Be Saved?" *The Nation* 17 June 2004, 19 June 2004. <http://www.thenation.com/doc. mhtml?i=20040705&c=5&s=forum1>.Commenting on same-sex marriage in the US, Bronski notes the gendered quality of the business: "Equally surprising to me is that, to a large degree, this [same-sex marriage] is a gendered affair. In fact, close to 75 percent of marriages that have taken place (legally) in Boston and (illegally) in San Francisco

have been between women. (In my extensive social and political circle of friends, I know of only two male couples who have decided to get hitched.) Clearly there is something about state-sanctioned marriage that is more appealing to lesbians, and probably women in general."

REFERENCES

Bronski, Michael. "Can Marriage Be Saved?" *The Nation* 17 June 2004. 19 June 2004. *http://www.thenation.com/doc.mhtml?i=20040705&c=5&s=forum1.*

Brown, Amy Benson. "Keeping Company, Staying Power, Keeping Power." *The Academic Exchange* Oct./Nov. 2002. 3 July 2004. *http://www.emory.edu/ACAD_EXCHANGE/ 2002/sept/keepingsidebar.html.*

"Collective Agreement between Queen's University Faculty Association and Queen's University at Kingston." Kingston, 2002. Queen's University. 21 May 2004. *http:// www.queensu.ca/qufa/Collective_Agreement/candx.htm.*

"Convention Collective Intervenue Entre L'uqam Et Le Seuqam." Montreal, 2002. UQAM. 19 May 2004. *http://www.rhu.uqam.ca/relationspro/Documents/Convention Seuqam.pdf.*

Davenport, Doris. "Still Here: Ten Years Later. . . ." *Tilting the Tower.* Ed. Linda Garber. New York & London: Routledge, 1999. 215-26.

Duggan, Lisa. "The New Homonormativity: The Sexual Politics of Neoliberalism. *Materializing Democracy: Toward a Revitalized Cultural Politics.* Ed. Russ Castronovo and Dana D. Nelson. Durham: Duke University Press, 2002. 175-94.

_____. *The Twilight of Equality: Neoliberalism, Cultural Politics, and the Attack on Democracy.* Boston: Beacon Press, 2003.

Gallop, Jane. *Feminist Accused of Sexual Harrassment.* Durham: Duke University Press, 1997.

_____. "Resisting Reasonableness." *Anecdotal Theory.* Durham: Duke University Press, 2002. 67-80.

Graff, E.J. *What Is Marriage For? The Strange Social History of Our Most Intimate Institution.* 1999. Boston: Beacon Press. 2004.

Klages, Mary. "The Ins and Outs of a Lesbian Academic." *Tilting the Tower.* Ed. Linda Garber. New York & London: Routledge, 1999. 235-42.

Nadeau, Chantal. "Unruly Privileges, or La Loi Du Silence: Same-Sex Spousal Hiring in Academia." 3 Oct.1999. CULSTUD-L. *http://www.cas.usf.edu/communication/ rodman/cultstud/columns.html.*

Nemoto, Shino, and Toren Finkel. "Ageing and the Mystery at Earles." *Nature: an international weekly journal of science* 429 (2004): 149.

QUFA Bargaining Committee Queen's University. 2000. 20 May 2004. *http:// www.queensu.ca/qufa/Negotiations_Archives/Negotiations_2001-02/Settlement_2002- 05.htm.*

Rees, Ruth. "Equity in Faculty Recruitment." *International Electronic Journal For Leadership in Learning* 28 Sept. 2000. 19 May 2004. *http://www.acs.ucalgary.ca/ ~iejll/volume4/rees_v4n12.html.*

Ristock, Janice L., and Catherine G. Taylor, eds. *Inside academia and Out: Lesbian/ Gay/Queer Studies and Social Action.* Toronto: University of Toronto Press, 1998.

Rubin, Gayle. "Thinking Sex: Notes for a Radical Theory of the Politics of Sexuality." *The Lesbian and Gay Studies Reader*. Eds. Henry Abelove, Michèle Aina Barale and David M. Halperin. New York: Routledge, 1993. 3-44. 1984.

"University of Victoria Federal Contractors Program Compliance Review Report 1993-2003." Victoria, B.C., 2003. University of Victoria. *http://web.uvic.ca/equity/FCP2003/Part1.pdf.*

Warner, Michael. *The Trouble with Normal: Sex Politics, and the the Ethics of Queer Life*. 1999. Cambridge, Massachusetts: Harvard University Press, 2000.

Wilson, Robin. "A Couple's Struggle to Find Good Jobs in the Same City: He's at Yale; She's at Missouri; and the Humanities Job Market Makes Their Search a Challenge." *Chronicle of Higher Education* April 2000. 21 May 2004. *http://chronicle.com/free/v46/i33/33a00101.htm.*

———. "When Officemates Are Also Roommates." *The Chronicle of Higher Education* (1998): A12, A13.

Performing Transformation:
Reflections of a Lesbian Academic Couple

Michelle Gibson
Deborah T. Meem

University of Cincinnati

SUMMARY. We experience queer literacy as a kind of collision between the traditional and the transformative. Queer literacy is an acquired literacy of transformation, where the established rules of behavior and discourse are both challenged and transcended. As a lesbian academic couple in a privileged intellectual, political, and social location, we can move out of the traditional realm (through the closet) into an otherworldly queer space where knowledge and identity are

---

Michelle Gibson is Associate Professor of English and Women's Studies at the University of Cincinnati. She has published poetry and scholarly work in the areas of composition studies and cultural studies, including "The Peculiar Case of Contessa" (*Transformations*, 2004) and co-editing with Jonathan Alexander a special cluster on Queer Theory for *Journal of Advanced Composition* (2004). With Deb Meem she co-edited *Femme/Butch: New Considerations of the Way We Want to Go* (Haworth, 2002).

Deborah T. Meem is Professor of English and Women's Studies at the University of Cincinnati. She has edited Eliza Lynn Linton's novel *The Rebel of the Family* (Broadview, 2002) and published in literary and cultural studies. With Michelle Gibson and Martha Marinara she wrote "Bi, Butch, and Bar Dyke: Pedagogical Performances of Class, Gender, and Sexuality" (*CCC*, 2000), and she and Gibson have collaborated on other articles on butch-femme lesbian gender.

[Haworth co-indexing entry note]: "Performing Transformation: Reflections of a Lesbian Academic Couple." Gibson, Michelle, and Deborah T. Meem. Co-published simultaneously in *Journal of Lesbian Studies* (Harrington Park Press, an imprint of The Haworth Press, Inc.) Vol. 9, No. 4, 2005, pp. 107-128; and: *Lesbian Academic Couples* (ed: Michelle Gibson, and Deborah T. Meem) Harrington Park Press, an imprint of The Haworth Press, Inc., 2005, pp. 107-128. Single or multiple copies of this article are available for a fee from The Haworth Document Delivery Service [1-800-HAWORTH, 9:00 a.m. - 5:00 p.m. (EST). E-mail address: docdelivery@haworthpress.com].

Available online at http://www.haworthpress.com/web/JLS
doi:10.1300/J155v9n04_08

destabilized. Moving in and out of queer transformative space requires a kind of blind faith–faith that believes in what the mind can neither see nor prove. *[Article copies available for a fee from The Haworth Document Delivery Service: 1-800-HAWORTH. E-mail address: <docdelivery@ haworthpress.com> Website: <http://www.HaworthPress.com> © 2005 by The Haworth Press, Inc. All rights reserved.]*

KEYWORDS. Lesbian, academic couple, collaboration, queer

It may be that what is "right" and what is "good" consist in staying open to the tensions that beset the most fundamental categories we require, to know unknowingness at the core of what we know, and what we need, and to recognize the sign of life–and its prospects.

–Judith Butler, *Undoing Gender*

Our relationship begins in work–scholarship, workaday interactions with colleagues and students, teaching, we do all of this together. We begin our day together, we eat breakfast and prepare lunches together, we fill our coffee mugs together, we get in the car and drive to the office together. Our offices, in fact, are in the same suite, and through all of our relationship we have worked no more than a few feet away from each other. It's frightening how "connected" we are, how similar our lives are, and we know the degree of privilege that gives us. Ironically, though, much of our collaborative scholarship has focused not on the similarities between us, but on the differences, because most of the collaborative work we have done has been about the way our genders impact our relationships to colleagues and students. It's a funny, fuzzy line we cross every time we write one of those pieces, though, because we are (as we illustrate above) much more similar than we are different. It's not uncommon for someone to whom we are being introduced to turn to whichever one of us is the second to be introduced and say, "So how about you? What do you do?" The answer, no matter which one of us is answering, is usually, "The same thing as her, in the same department, just down the hall, in fact."

What differentiates us from each other–and the issue we have discussed so frequently in our work together–has to do with our angle of vision. Deb sees herself as a butch lesbian (though not identifying as such until she and Michelle began their romance) and Michelle sees herself as a femme lesbian (though not identifying as such until she was introduced to the concept as an aspect of sexual play). If these categories sound essentialist, that's because both Deb and Michelle experience them that way, to some extent at least. Deb is happy to show the picture of herself wearing a cowboy hat and a low-slung pistol holster on the afternoon of her third birthday. Michelle counters with the photo of herself in a frilly new green dress given by her grandmother. So, you ask, does this mean that both Deb and Michelle have *always* been butch and femme? Let's return to the photos. Wild West Deb has shoulder-length blonde curls, and wears a lacy white blouse tucked into her jeans. Fashion Plate Michelle sports a pixie haircut, suitable for tomboy activities. Somehow our butch-femme "identities" are clouded by inconsistencies—we just can't pull off the essentialist thing. Deb may correctly see her child self as out of step with the 1950s imperative for girly-girls, and Michelle may remember that vision in green as an experience of comfort through style. And in fact, today's crew-cut Deb may watch the Super Bowl, while coiffed and lipsticked Michelle visits Bath & Body Works. The gendered differences between us seem to us to be more constructed than essential. So we fancy ourselves queer to the core, and at the same time we acknowledge the fluid, unsubstantial, performed nature of that queerness.

To say that queer is a destabilizing identity category is not new, but a central tenet of the major works of queer theory over the last two decades. Indeed, Annamarie Jagose writes, "Acknowledging the inevitable violence of identity politics and having no stake in its own hegemony, queer is less an identity than a *critique* of identity" (131). Which brings us to our point: as queers contained within and seeing through our sexed bodies and culture, we are engaged in a constant (some would say tiresome) queer critique. Our dinner-table chatter often focuses on questions and commentary about the way our gendered performances are received by those around us or on the way the performances of those around us reflect or refuse to reflect our sense of ourselves as gender performers. We are fascinated by the quality of vision from our different vantage points, particularly when it comes to ostensibly shared experiences and relationships. Our genders thus enhance the quality of our romantic relationship because they foreground and intensify the differences in lives most characterized by similarity. At the same time we recognize a gendered quality in the way others—and here we refer specifically to our colleagues at the university—see us. Our butch and femme self-presentations, which we have deliberately chosen to perform in spite of some evidence that these are "identities"

innate to us, govern the way our peers relate to us in various settings
on campus. Herein lies the paradox. Others approach us as if our
butch and femme demeanors were permanent and unchanging–or
(and?) we explain their responses to us in those terms. On the one hand,
then, we experience our genders (variable and fluctuating as they might
be) as essential in that they function as lenses through which we interpret others' behavior. On the other hand, though, we experience gender
as playful and performative, liminal and shifting, essential and constructed, interior and exterior.

This kind of queer critique is both *infallible*, because it reframes the
world not to reach definitive conclusions but to allow for clearer vision,
and *fallible*, because it is filtered through the inconsistent, chaotic human psyche where all that *is* simultaneously *is not*, where construction
and deconstruction are simultaneous, and where there is no consistently
identifiable line between fact and fiction. And because we are an academic couple, constantly engaged in (what some would call) inane conversation about (what some would call) esoteric ideas, this phenomenon
in which our critiques simultaneously are and are not accurate is at least
doubled in intensity–queers queering the queered. We urge readers to
move beyond what seems to be the logical conclusion–that our vision is
merely blurred by these queer inconsistencies–and to consider the possibility that the complexity of our critique also clarifies our vision. It's a
kind of psychic intensifying of one sense in the absence of another.

Let us explore how this intensification operates. When gender is dis-
connected from chromosomal sex and displaced from masculine and
feminine conceived as polar opposites, butch and femme explode into
prismatic variety. According to this way of perceiving gender, a butch's
womanness is only one refraction of the prism through which she sees
the world. Butch and femme are not masculine and feminine displaced
onto woman, but additional kaleidoscopic patterns generated by queer
gender. We access these disordered/disorderly fragments of vision
through interpellation–through consciously figuring ourselves as inhabiting an *inter*space between the cultural binaries. Like Lewis
Carroll's Alice, like C.S. Lewis's Lucy, like J.K. Rowling's Harry Potter, we approach borderland "portals" seeking to understand what is beyond. In *Through the Looking-Glass*, Alice uses "mirror" vision to
cross into "queer" space; upon arriving, she finds that she can read in-
verted writing–that is, a "Looking-glass book" (95)–by holding it up to
the "glass" through which she has just passed. Alice, in other words,
gains knowledge of "inversion" through "reflecting" upon the straight
world turned inside out. In *The Lion, the Witch, and the Wardrobe*,

Lucy finds her way to Narnia via a wardrobe, which opens out into the fantasy kingdom. Conceived alternatively, Lucy uses the closet to access queer space; the closet thus becomes the gateway to queer knowledge, and ultimately, a kind of power. Harry Potter, in *Harry Potter and the Sorcerer's Stone*, must find Track Nine and Three-Quarters in order to board the train for the Hogwarts School of Witchcraft and Wizardry. There is no entrance to this magical land through whole numbers; only the space in the middle allows passage. So Harry can only enter queer space–specifically queer intellectual space–by navigating between the poles of "normal" understanding and capability (Gates Nine and Ten), and by trusting that what looks like a concrete wall is really a passageway that will admit him if he believes it will. Alice, Lucy, and Harry symbolize for us three interconnected and roughly sequential processes that obtain in our lives as partners in a butch-femme identified academic couple: literacy, power, and faith.

THE BOOK IN THE MIRROR: READING FROM A QUEER SPACE

Alice's discovery of how to read her new space is the beginning of her ability to understand it. Like Alice, we learn through the practice of "reading" our academic world as "inverts," i.e., as queers inhabiting a fluid and contested gender location. We find that we interpret situations based on "reading" other people and their reactions in terms of how gender operates. Just like everyone else, when we leave the world we call "home" each morning we enter a world where literacy is constantly redefined–by interaction. At home, because we are the only two people living there, we are fairly literate in that we are familiar with each other's possible interpretations of events, comments, etc. But when we pass through the looking glass and into the more complex world teeming with people whose interpretations we cannot imagine, whether or not we are able to read depends on whether the context in which that reading occurs remains consistent. When the context changes we are screwed–at least until we learn to read in the language of the new context. Let us offer an example.

During the years 2002-2004, the University of Cincinnati underwent a painful restructuring, which ultimately involved the closing of the two open-admissions units on the main campus. Faculty members from these two units were reassigned to other departments in the university. This reassignment was handled badly, and transferring faculty were

subjected to a humiliating process of review by the receiving departments, whose members insisted upon interviewing transferees, ostensibly to ensure the best possible "fit," but in reality, assuming that
receiving department members were superior scholars, sometimes to
find reasons to reject people they did not deem worthy. Michelle and
Deb and three others were transferred into the English Department in
the College of Arts & Sciences, and we should say that our experience
was better than that of many of our former colleagues. Nevertheless, the
transfer was not without problems. Deb, a full professor, was offered a
lighter ("research") teaching load and advanced classes immediately.
Initially, Michelle and the others were assigned an additional class each
quarter, and restricted to 100-and 200-level courses.[1] The reason given
for this differential was rank–presumably Deb's advanced rank indicated that she had already "proven herself" in ways the others hadn't,
even though all but one were tenured associate professors.

We had come from a department where the environment was carefully constructed to avoid privileging rank over all else. While we understood that there should be some benefit to achieving advanced rank
and that it was important to the department's status in the rest of the university to have active full professors in the department and college, we
valued the tension new faculty brought to the department and we valued
the critique they engaged in on a daily basis. So, suddenly to be in a position where rank was one of the more important factors in determining
privilege surprised us, to say the least. We heard from friends who
worked in the department that some junior faculty believed that only
those who had earned the right through longevity felt able to speak in
department meetings, but we had no idea what the other rules of discourse (and power and privilege) might be in our new department.

What's more, because we had worked for so long in a department
where those who had achieved higher rank were not necessarily privileged and because we identify as feminists, we understand that academic rank is always already gendered, and privileging rank has
traditionally operated to disempower women in the academy. Barbara
Lee, Dean of the School of Management and Labor Relations at Rutgers
University, points out, "In 2003, women comprised 18.2 percent of full
professors at doctoral-granting universities" (Lee). If the rank of full
professor is dominated by men, then privileging rank is inherently sexist. Interestingly, the women professors in our new department who
were held to higher teaching loads and less prestigious teaching assignments for one year after the transfer are all women we would identify as
femme (two straight and two lesbian), and the one woman–Deb–who

was seen as having already passed muster identifies as butch. Privileging rank in this case allowed our receiving department to assume that its decision was reasonable, to be blissfully unaware of the sexism inherent in it. And that bliss was not interrupted when those making the decisions read us all as "female"; if we were all female, then there could be no sexism involved in offering benefits to one, could there? Among the department's longtime faculty, both women and men proceeded as though there were nothing to question in the practice of privileging rank in important decisions.

However, as a lesbian couple, both of whom are acutely aware of the way sexism functions, we "read" the situation as sexist and discussed that phenomenon at length. We came to realize that the whole rank-privileging practice was supported and complicated by Deb's butchness. In many ways, the men in the department were treating Deb as if she were "one of the guys." In light of this assumption, several men seemed surprised that Deb would speak out against what she saw as an unfair situation, and the department head asked Deb if she intended to give up her "research" teaching load and teach extra courses like the rest of the transferees. Would he have expected, or even thought it possible, that a man might consider such self-sacrifice in the service of a principle?

Clearly Deb's perceived "masculinity," both in itself and in her relationship to femme Michelle, marked her as a (potential) member of the power group and "earned" her privilege. At the same time, Deb's femaleness masked the sexism inherent in the unequal distribution of good things. Because butch gender simultaneously enacts male and female, it inhabits a space not easily imagined by non-queers, especially those whose access to power and privilege depends in part upon gender understood as a male-female binary. In this space, a butch can critique the very privilege offered to her, and she can perform that critique precisely because she is butch, i.e., gendered outside the blinding influence of polarized male and female.

But, you ask, might not the blinding work the other way round? Might we be *over*-reading, over-reaching, blinded to the possibility that things are no more than they are? Blinded to simplicity? Blinded to pure motives? We wrote above of a critique that is at once infallible by virtue of seeking clear vision rather than certain conclusions, and also fallible by virtue of inhabiting the fluctuating undefined space between genders. The literacy we claim lies not in what we know or can prove, but in that same liminal space of questioning and theorizing. This is a literacy of critique, not of answers. As such it is a feminist critique, concerned with process, not with product. We are tempted to impose a queer theoretical spin upon Ti-Grace Atkinson's familiar statement that "Feminism is the theory, lesbianism is the practice" (quoted in Koedt), for we can engage in the practice of queer critique precisely because second-wave feminists provided us with a foundational theory. But perhaps a more fruitful focus is Jill Johnston's tweaking of Atkinson: "Feminism at heart is a massive complaint. Lesbianism is the solution" (166). Johnston criticizes mainstream feminism on the grounds that straight feminists are too closely tied to men to engage in any radical refiguring of society. Lesbians, she writes, must always reject accommodationist agendas because we are not bound by self-interest to link our fortunes to men's. Our re-vision of Johnston arises from our recognition that our critique is both feminist and queer. We propose that, *contra* Sheila Jeffreys, queer (as opposed to LGBT) studies need not be "feminism-free" (459). As feminists, we do "complain" of perceived injustices perpetrated upon women as a group. But our queerness, and specifically our butch-femme genders, lead us into the "solution," the bubbling brew of prismatic identity fragments that enables us to achieve a kind of literacy of resistance. We refuse to be limited by the idea of accuracy, since the concept "accurate" depends on the right/wrong binary. Our queer space transcends, for instance, the male/female binary; we must not allow it to be influenced by other constraining ethical bookends. Critique is a process, not a product, and those willing to truly engage in it are also willing to float around in the space between the binary poles of right and wrong.

THROUGH THE CLOSET:
ACCESS TO POWER AND PRIVILEGE

The notion that queers "come out" of the closet, while useful in a rights-based discourse, finally limits queers in that it implies that we emerge into a space that already exists, that we assimilate into that space, that the inhabitants of that space have the authority to deem us worthy or unworthy of interaction with them. We like to think of ourselves as having come *through* the closet in the way that the four children in *The Lion, the Witch, and the Wardrobe* enter Narnia bearing their earthly knowledge. When we enter the ostensibly straight space of the university, the academic department, the classroom, we do so equipped with our queerness, insisting all the time on our right to infuse the environment with it. We intend not only to mingle among the inhab-

itants, but to affect them in some ways. As Harriet Malinowitz writes in
Textual Orientations,

> I'm not hovering at that threshold of indecision where the bene-
> fits of being out can be swiftly weighed against the liabilities. I'm
> already out; when I walk into this room it's into an existing dis-
> course that I have already instigated. And so I proceed with the
> freedom to say what I want, my trajectory unweighted by fears of
> repercussions and hopes that my silence will protect me. (xv)

Malinowitz imagines the space on the other side of the closet as alive
with a kind of queer power–"outness" already accomplished, fears and
hesitations minimized, and queer discourse possible, even validated by
the community at large. As a lesbian academic couple (as opposed to
two lesbian individuals), we represent a kind of embodied presence that
occupies intellectual, political, and social space. When a lesbian is in a
Curriculum Committee meeting, when she is teaching "Introduction to
Poetry" or "History of the Novel," when she is chatting with colleagues
in the hallway, her sexuality can be invisible or constructed as inciden-
tal to who she is "on the job"–particularly if it's not necessarily her job
to be queer (as it would be the work of an LGBT scholar to be queer).
But when a lesbian academic couple works together in the same department, they are constantly enacting queerness–even in those situations
that might not seem to allow for enacting queerness. A couple's embodiment of sex and sexuality is much more consistently visible than an
individual's. A lesbian or *a* gay man can be absorbed into the surrounding culture with nary a ripple. But a couple is a living reminder that
queers exist in numbers, that they may represent a significant point of
view or set of experiences tangential to, if not opposed to, the mainstream. A couple is seen as a force, and thus has the privilege of consistent practice. In other words, because Michelle and Deb participate in
departmental life as a couple, we are never expected to justify or explain
our individual lesbian lives; instead, we assume the privilege of being
already recognized, and in turn this privilege leads to power. There is a
social power in being a couple, of course; but more than this, we find it
easy to use the existing structures of the university to our advantage
simply on account of operating together within them.

• We push for, and succeed in implementing, a Sexuality Studies
  track within the Women's Studies major; we operate a clearing-
  house of LGBT-related courses on campus.

- Thus we collaborate in bringing Sexuality Studies forward as a visible and valued field of intellectual inquiry.
- Thus, because our departments (English and Women's Studies) recognize this work, we can co-author this article and count it toward our institutional advancement.
- Thus we gain privilege and power within the institution, at least partly on account of being a couple.

Here we see how the *academic* part of "lesbian academic couple" operates to our advantage. On a global level, we are privileged that our institution protects academic freedom and values a wide variety of approaches to knowledge. On a more local level, we benefit from the fact that queerness–in person and as a field of study–is generally seen as an accepted area of inquiry in English departments, and as part of the basic foundation of Women's Studies. And of course, discrimination against LGBT people is seen as both un-hip and immoral in these environments.

As we experience it, the land in which we live and work is an otherworldly space where queerness is ever-present, where it empowers rather than disempowers us. And, while our emotional and psychic energy is focused on other lesbians–academic or not–we are aware that we have much more in common experientially with our straight academic colleagues than with, say, the lesbians who run Camp Sister Spirit in Ovett, Mississippi.

> Since November 1993, lesbian partners Wanda & Brenda Henson, along with numerous volunteers, have defended their 120 acre "Camp Sister Spirit" folkschool from an ongoing, religious-right-inspired campaign of violence, harassment, intimidation and death threats. There have been over 64 incidents to date, including telephone death threats, mail-bomb threats, explosives at their gate and a dead dog tied to their mailbox. (Tyler)

Like the Hensons, we are a lesbian couple doing lesbian work, and like the Hensons, we see our work as educational, as residing in a specific space (a "folkschool" for them, a university for us), and like the Hensons, we have been the subject of right-wing attempts at intimidation. But our experiences are simply not comparable to theirs. When a "Safe Zone" sticker with a pink triangle on it is defaced to read "Moron Zone," when "Faggot" is scrawled across a poster on an office door, when an operative from Accuracy in Academe[2] dogs our movements at conferences and then shows up and takes copious notes at a queer mini-conference on campus–these are annoyances, to be sure. But unlike the Hensons, we do not sleep with rifles by our sides. Despite the University of Cincinnati's conservative Board of Trustees, despite the city's white Republican bigotry, our university is a sanctuary, a progressive oasis in a region parched of tolerance. We are intensely aware of our privilege in being able to do the work we do with few personal sacrifices required. In fact, when our scholarship brings us into contact with queer colleagues from small conservative liberal arts colleges and other institutions where they are in their daily lives asked (either by fiat or by suggestion) to remain closeted in one way or another, we are reminded that the kind of privilege we enjoy is still quite localized in this country, and more specifically in US academe. At meetings of the Caucus of LGBT Professionals (held annually at the Conference on College Composition and Communication), we have encountered dozens of faculty members working at other institutions who simply cannot come out. For them it is not a question of testing their rights or seeking acceptance from their colleagues; there are no rights, no presumption of connection. If they do come out–in their scholarship, in their classrooms, in their personal lives–they place themselves in real danger. Ed Madden, for example, describes his article "Immersive Pedagogies" as a "risky essay" (1), partly because he wishes to avoid slipping into "sensationalism and sentimentality," but also because its subject matter has already led a conservative journalist in Columbia, South Carolina, to out him publicly, even printing his home address. Madden perseveres in spite of the risk; Michelle and Deb have so far been immune to such intimidation. But we are far from relaxing. Madden describes student complaints that his course entitled "Literature and AIDS" was too political. During the 2005-2006 Regular Session of the Ohio General Assembly, legislators will consider S.B. No. 24, an "academic bill of rights" clearly intended to muzzle liberal voices in the academy, and undermine academic freedom ("As Introduced"). State Senator Larry Mumper of Marion, the primary sponsor of the bill, told a reporter for *The Columbus Dispatch* that "80 percent or so of [professors] are Democrats, liberals or socialists or card-carrying Communists" who are attempting to brainwash students (Hallett). If Mumper's bill passes, what will become of Sexuality Studies courses at Cincinnati? Will our privilege and power be jeopardized?

This brings us back to the otherworldliness of our privilege. Even when the "world" out there looks particularly ominous, we realize that in important ways we are protected. We learned about the academic bill of rights not from LGBT activists or IndyMedia, but from our department head, who circulated it in an e-mail to all English faculty. That same department head asked Michelle about her response to the recent anti-gay marriage amendment in Ohio, the day after the election. He was clearly distressed by what he saw as a patently unfair and homophobic result. A colleague of ours, a woman recently widowed, was talking to us about dating. Without hesitation, Michelle asked whether she had considered dating women. Her response was something like, "I've considered it, but I don't think that's where I am." Our friendship with this faculty member, and her consistent support of our relationship (both to each other and to her), made that conversation feel easy and natural. We mention these incidents because they illustrate how in our work environment we are insulated by straight people who are not merely allies, but who are willing to function as friends in a space where the boundary between straight and queer is constantly negotiated and renegotiated. We remember that the four adventurous children in *The Lion, the Witch, and the Wardrobe* are unlikely heroes in their everyday world, precisely because they are children. But when they go through the closet they can be heroes, because the Narnia-world around them permits it. At our university, Michelle and Deb and two other queers can sit with President Nancy Zimpher and discuss domestic partner benefits, precisely because we have left our closets behind us, and we carry with us the support of our colleagues, who believe in our cause. In fact, the extent of that support diminishes the need for us to behave heroically. Ultimately, heroic feats are performed less by individuals than by the communities that back them; we are very cognizant of the friendly cushion our colleagues provide for us.

RUNNING AT THE WALL: FAITH AND CONTESTED IDENTITIES

To catch the train to Hogwarts School, Harry Potter must run at full speed, pushing a cart holding all his belongings, toward a concrete wall where Track Nine and Three-Quarters must be. Any hesitation–any weakening of his faith in its existence–and Harry will suffer a painful collision. If that occurs, he will be stuck in the land of Muggles (nonmagical people) who don't acknowledge his power as a Wizard; he will also be physically bruised. Harry must behave as if the passageway exists, for Hogwarts is his community. Like Harry Potter, we have learned that access to queer/liminal space requires faith, and like Harry Potter we understand that if we don't catch the train to the "other world" we will be trapped in our own sense of disbelonging, of problematic difference, and we expect that our distinct and special view of the world will be rejected in favor of a discourse in which sameness, not transformation, is the goal. Moreover, we observe that behaving *as if that space exists* is already transformative.

The looking-glass, the closet, the concrete wall–whatever we name the hard material that divides "straight" space from "queer" space–the process of moving through that apparently unyielding surface is a daunting task. It may involve partial or unsuccessful attempts; it may involve reproof, coercion, ostracism, medical intervention, incarceration, even physical injury. But many queer people understand that it is less the visibility than the silence that equals death. Outness has been shown to correlate positively with psychological health,[3] even when being out only means linking up with an isolated and endangered queer community in hostile territory. A lesbian academic couple–in safe circumstances such as those we enjoy–has the privilege of moving fairly easily through coming-out into a condition of living-out. The scary process still obtains, of course; we must burst through the barrier of real or fancied homophobia (carrying all our "baggage") into the queer space beyond. But the nature of that space feels different from the defended outness of the Hensons in Ovett, Mississippi, or even our colleagues at other institutions for whom coming out could mean loss of their jobs. For them, being out means battling for survival in a contested space defined by straightness. By contrast, our academic queer space is potentially pliable, magical, welcoming, celebratory. In our work environment, we are not dependent upon tolerance or acceptance by others who define the terms of our outness. Instead we inhabit a genuinely queer environment where we set those terms *with* straights. Here all identities are potentially contested; yet the contestedness of the space is a positive attribute, both for us and for our colleagues who do not identify as queer. Because we are not in danger, we have the luxury of not having to ask for a "safe" space to be queer. In fact, we prefer that the space *not* be safe; we want the notion of identity always to be contested. We refuse to ask for the right to exist, or the right to speak; we insist on creating a sense of identity that is always in flux because it is always contested. We see this *lack* of safety as the goal; we don't want straight folks feeling safe in their heterosexism, and by the same token we don't want to replace heterosexism with "homosexism" or some other essentialist reality. The queer environment we value is one where safety is relinquished in favor of multiplicity. We believe, with Nikki Sullivan, that "a critique of single-axis

accounts of identity is integral to the queering of humanism more generally (and vice versa), and thus of heteronormativity" (73). This space is
marked not by the goal of achieving, for instance, tolerance, but by a
willingness to reside in a state of flux. We are describing not a transformed space, but a space always in the process of transforming. Let us
now talk about this as lived experience.

   In 1994, when Michelle was hired to teach English in the open-access
day college at the University of Cincinnati, she came into a department
that was visibly queer. In fact, one way the search committee "courted"
her was by sending the *three* queer members of the search committee to
the LGBT Caucus meeting she co-chaired at the conference where her
initial interview took place. But in spite of that visibility, the department
was conventional and, at least on the surface, mostly heterosexual, because the two gay men (a third had recently retired at that time) were, if
not closeted, at least quietly low-key about their sexuality. The other
lesbian aside from Deb was fairly new to the department, and, though
out to anyone who cared to know, was not inclined to make waves.
Michelle's vita contained many references to her lesbianism; it was
clear that hiring her meant hiring an out queer who expected to continue
being out wherever she ended up. At that time, Deb was the only faculty
member on campus who was teaching courses in LGBT Studies. Our
decision to become romantic partners two years later thus brought together two insistently out lesbians. This decision had a visible impact on
our friends and colleagues in the department. The department chair (a
friend of ours) called one evening to tell Deb that there had been "rumors" that we had begun seeing each other. We were, at the very moment when the phone call came, negotiating between ourselves the level
of visibility we wanted our relationship to have in our day-to-day work
lives, so on the spur of the moment we confirmed that the rumors were
true and let the chips fall where they may.

   Mostly, our colleagues began instantly to try to understand our relationship as part of the landscape. Those to whom we were emotionally
close often relayed information about comments made by those who
wondered whether the romance might make us "too powerful" by giving us incentive to "vote as a bloc," and our chair made clear that Deb
(who was Michelle's senior colleague) could not serve in any capacity
that involved her evaluating Michelle's work. Rumor has it that one colleague wondered whether Deb's involvement with Michelle might be
considered "sexual harassment" and accused Michelle of sleeping her
way to the top. Reading us in terms of our butch and femme genders,
this colleague constructed Deb as the lecherous male interested in little

beyond satisfying her own (insatiable?) sexual appetite, and Michelle as the conniving female subordinate using her sexuality in place of hard work to advance. Ironically, this construction doesn't work in our academic environment where the line between superior and subordinate is often blurred and where advancement does not depend on personal favor so much as on meeting "the criteria" for reappointment, promotion, and tenure set forth in the contract negotiated by the AAUP and the university administration. We are fairly convinced that this colleague was responding to our genders rather than our lesbianism because of her reaction to another (straight) couple in the department. If the rumors are accurate, she constructed the male in that relationship in much the same way as she constructed Deb, and the female in much the same way as she constructed Michelle. This kind of excessive focus on butch-as-male (including all the power that gender position can entail) can elide femme gender, which partakes on the surface of traditionally "feminine" appearance and behaviors. While a butch woman is visible in the world *as* a lesbian, the femme can be at once assumed to be straight (by straights) and viewed askance as a "failed" or "lesser" lesbian (by queers). In general, Deb is perceived as the dyke-on-campus. She is the one students ask to attend LGBTQ functions, or that they seek out for information on queer courses and organizations. We are convinced that this is true only because she is butch and looks like the stereotypical lesbian. And it has been true no matter how prominent a role Michelle has played in queer activities on campus; even when Michelle was faculty advisor to the student LGBTQ Alliance, students and faculty looked to Deb when they wanted a lesbian presence. In an amusing example of this phenomenon, even another lesbian faculty member (herself a femme!) announced a meeting of the faculty LGBT Task Force "at Deb's house," as if Michelle was invisible. (To her credit, this faculty member was mortified when she realized what she had done.)

For us, butch and femme may partake of innate impulses to some extent, but in our living of these gender positionalities, we choose to emphasize the ways butch and femme genders are artificial, performative, visible . . . and thus, camp. Camp has traditionally functioned as a core aspect of queer aesthetics, and butch-femme camp in particular seems to have emerged from what Sue-Ellen Case calls "the feminist closet" during the so-called Sex Wars of the 1980s. Case writes that "the closet has given us camp–the style, the discourse, the *mise en scène* of butch-femme roles" (297). Camp represents a heightened gender performance, a use of drag to produce an effect that is at once core and surface. We use the term "drag" here in Judith Butler's sense, i.e., that drag "constitutes the mundane way in which genders are appropriated, theatricalized, worn, and done; it implies that all gendering is a kind of impersonation and approximation" (313). Having come through the closet, we put on butch-femme drag and enact butch-femme camp as part of our interaction with our colleagues. We use these tools deliberately to highlight gender, to foreground difference. For example, one of Michelle's good friends in the access-college department was a woman who is straight in terms of her declared sexuality, but high femme in terms of her performed gender. A significant part of their relationship hinges upon the humorous enactment of femme–including femme bonding "against" butch (lack of) style. One day this colleague complimented Michelle on a new blouse. Michelle responded, "Deb says it looks like a maternity blouse." The colleague huffed and answered, "Now you are taking fashion advice from a woman who wears Birkenstocks with socks all winter long?" In this case, a person who identifies as straight has become familiar with queer gender camp; her participation in a friendship with Michelle involves her entrance into queer space. Having observed campy gendered banter between Deb and Michelle, and more generally among all the queer faculty in the department, she understands the discursive mode and can use it to deepen the intimacy of the friendship without stumbling into offensive territory. What's more, she has faith that we will not take offense, but will re-establish discursive boundaries when necessary. She thus has the freedom to test the limits of gender identification with humor and affection. Her comfort level with femme camp was revealed recently when she gave Michelle a birthday card, already featuring a kind of (hetero)sexual innuendo, which she had altered to reflect the existing differences between their stated sexual preferences. The card's original conversation between two straight women thus morphed into a hilarious repartee between a "straight girl" and a "gay girl." The nature of the relationship between Michelle and this colleague illustrates first, how humor functions to enable interactions in potentially risky space, and second, how the faith that gets queers through the closet creates possibilities for new types of gender play, and new players.

For us, an important way of behaving as if we inhabit a queered space has been to inject humor into our personal interactions at the university. We are mindful of the way(s) that what psychologists call "healthful humor" has been assumed to help build relationships. "In general," writes Steve Sultanoff, "healthful humor stimulates wit, mirth, or laughter. It creates closeness and intimacy. . . . Often healthful humor pokes fun at oneself and situations" (*http://www.aath.org/aath_qa.html*). As we implied above, one effect of our heightened gender self-presentation is to call attention to the funny aspects of gender in general. Our notion that a space can be queered through the use of humor is not like the idea that self-deprecating humor defuses hostility. Instead, it focuses humor on the tension where differences collide, understanding that those tensions are productive. Specifically they are productive in that meeting them head on moves relationships forward. A group of our friends, all of whom became acquainted through interactions at work, have for the past several years been celebrating group birthdays with white elephant gift exchange parties. The group, made up of half queers and half straight people, centers its interactions almost entirely on the giving of gendered humorous gifts: a pink feathered tiara, "pecker" pasta, Valentine boxer shorts, a tin of breath mints with a studly half-naked man on the lid. What has led to this pattern is that the tension around difference in this mixed group is seen as a source of humor rather than defensiveness.

It is important to point out that none of these examples of productive queer interactions occurred after deep self-revelatory conversations. The space was queered because individuals had faith that it could happen, and acted accordingly. We live in a culture which contains few models for that kind of behavior between queers and straights–in other words, people being truly at ease with difference. We are so laden with a kind of therapeutic sense of how relationships work that emotional self-disclosure has become the model for establishing intimacy, and that model simply doesn't work, at least not initially, in most professional environments. Thus the notion that coming out is often–even typically– a drama-infused, earth-shattering experience. What we would argue is that there are ways of maintaining a faith in the possibility of *living out* that can in some environments be much more transformative than constantly engaging in the act of *coming out*. Time and again we have seen queers we know behave defensively in the presence of straights whom they believe are going to judge their every word and deed. What we have come to believe is that our own faith that that judgment won't occur has either made it not happen or has shielded us from the awareness of its happening. This is what we mean when we say that in many ways we have very little in common with queers who live in dangerous spaces.

Over the past few years, we have noticed that conference programs list fewer and fewer "lesbian and gay" topics–and we even think we see some decrease in the number of "queer" topics (although queer denotes a theoretical stance and methodology that still possess some charm for academics). We assume that this is happening not because academics are returning to McCarthyesque homophobia, but rather because queerness is gradually being integrated into other kinds of discussions. It is this very integration of queerness into academic life that we have related to the idea of faith–the faith that allows Harry Potter to charge into a concrete pillar, the faith that we define as moving forward *as if* the world we dream about already exists.

CONCLUSION:
TENSION, PARADOX, AND TRANSFORMATION

Living out as a lesbian academic couple is rife with a kind of chaotic synergy. We are aware that we experience considerable privilege in a day-to-day context, but that that privilege occurs in a university where simple rights-based activism is met with resistance by a conservative Board of Trustees, with whom even the argument of fiscal expediency doesn't hold sway. It occurs in a city which for a decade boasted of being the only one in the US that had successfully dodged the Supreme Court by enacting an Article in the City Charter which specifically excluded queers from protection from discrimination in housing and employment, and even forbade City Council from acting to institute such protections. It occurs in a state which in 2004 passed the most restrictive Defense of Marriage amendment of any in the country, and which is now among those considering a hare-brained "academic bill of rights" in its General Assembly. And it occurs in a nation where a (scant) majority have elected a president and a Congress whose party machinery has already set out to dismantle Affirmative Action, freedom of speech, environmental protections, welfare, and the separation of church and state. We believe that there is a quality of confrontation to the mere existence of a lesbian academic couple presenting themselves. Thus, in a way, our coupleness makes our resistance to the status quo more visible. We deliberately enact this resistance as a couple, because we understand that self-presentation as intensifying our political and social positionality.

In writing about lesbian academic couples, we have set out to confront four myths that have been used to disempower others like us:

1. With the religious right (we hope, temporarily) ascendant in this country, queers have been marked as without values, or representing the lack or loss of values.
2. Many institutions and/or businesses assume that couples working together in the same place are less productive than individuals,

particularly because they bring emotional issues, personal likes and dislikes, and a "power of two" into the workplace.

3. Couples in the workplace are generally (treated as) a husband and a wife, with the "wife" occupying a supportive, subordinate, but not fully participating space.

4. In our culture, it is commonly believed that a romantic relationship between two people precludes their also functioning effectively as friends, colleagues, and/or collaborators at work.

For us, scholarship and teaching are values. As academics, our family life and our university life revolve around intellectual work and intellectual play. We value the life of the mind–and we value sharing it with students, colleagues, friends, and relatives. Our queerness is part of our "liberal" approach to the world, an approach characterized by questioning, acceptance, reason, and humanism. As we see it, queerness implies flux, multiplicity, destabilization of identities, and constant interrogation of what is; our point of view thus reflects a queer value system. Our discussion of accessing, inhabiting, and sharing a queer academic space has aimed to illustrate this value system at work in the academy. This same discussion was also designed to show ways that a couple may be productive in an academic workplace, not in spite of but sometimes because of being a couple. Given the queer value system described above, individuals in a couple relationship need not operate as a single unit; our feeling is that we have a responsibility as an academic couple not to use our two-ness as a weapon. If we have a quarrel in the car on the way to school, if one of us shares an irritation concerning another member of the department, these "couple" conversations must vanish on campus. While living out as a lesbian academic couple makes us productive in both a scholarly sense and a social "transformative" sense, we insist on autonomy as individuals in the workplace. This has meant working to complicate others' assumptions about our butch-femme self-identifications as paralleling traditional husband-wife power relations. It hasn't always been easy. Some men in our new department welcomed Michelle as if she was Deb's wife. Their unexamined assumption that Michelle functioned as a faculty wife in the same way several of their own wives did–that is, working at the university but in positions commanding less prestige, power, and salary than their husbands'–both amused and troubled us. It clarified for us the importance of confronting heteronormative figurings of the "male"/"female" binary, and brought home yet again the need for constant feminist intervention even in the academy, where one might think views of women's position would be more evolved and less stereotypical than elsewhere. It also made us see the extent to which we would have to combat notions of how personal relations operate. Our relationship as a couple is founded on the romantic attachment that brought us together in the first place. But, as we have commented to each other many times, we believe that our personal and academic friendship–our sharing of political, moral, and intellectual opinions– is so deep that we would be professional companions and collaborators whether or not we were in a romantic relationship. More than this, we try to create and participate in other such friendships and collaborations–in other words, to be open to close professional relationships that do not require life partnerships to exist. We have mentioned some of these in this article. For us, they serve several functions: they work against the assumption that a couple must be a private twosome impervious to admittance of others; they allow for productive collaborations beyond just the two of us; and they permit us to inhabit highly charged queer spaces where identities are both celebrated and contested.

This brings us back to the notion of queer literacy, which we experience as a kind of collision between the traditional and the transformative. We understand that most of the time, people operate in the world using an inherited literacy based on society's traditional rules of behavior and discourse. Queer literacy, by contrast, is an acquired literacy of transformation, where the established rules of behavior and discourse are both challenged and transcended. As a lesbian academic couple in a privileged intellectual, political, and social location, we can move out of the traditional realm (through the closet) into an otherworldly queer space where knowledge and identity are destabilized. We can then re-emerge as necessary, carrying re-imagined relationships and structures. Moving in and out of queer transformative space requires a kind of blind faith–faith that believes in what the mind can neither see nor prove. This scary but necessary concept is what finally permits us access to space where our very queerness is a source of power, and the old world is transformed.

NOTES

1. We want to make clear that the teaching load and course level issues are now resolved, and by the beginning of our second year in the English Department, all of us had the same status as other members of the department.

2. Accuracy in Academe is a right-wing organization that "monitors" university professors and activities perceived to be liberal. The organization is one of many that appeared in the 1970s and 1980s in response to corporate attorney (later Supreme Court

justice) Lewis F. Powell's 1971 memo calling on American business to fight back against liberal attacks. A number of conservative foundations and think tanks arose, which in turn fund more specialized groups like Accuracy in Academe (Burns).

3. See, for instance, Eliason, "Identity Formation for Lesbian, Bisexual, and Gay Persons: Beyond a 'Minoritizing' View"; Falco, "Lesbian Identity Formation"; Margolies et al., "Internalized Homophobia: Identifying and Treating the Oppressor Within"; Herek et al., "Correlates of Internalized Homophobia in a Community Sample of Lesbians and Gay Men."

REFERENCES

"As Introduced." *126th Ohio General Assembly 2005-2006. S.B. No. 24. http://www.legislature.state.oh.us/bills.cfm?ID=126_SB_24*. 1 February 2005.

Burns, Margie. "Academia, business and government: the lucrative triangle in right-wing propaganda." *Online Journal*. 1 February 2005. *http://www.onlinejournal. com/Special_Reports/012805Burns/012805burns.html*.

Butler, Judith. "Imitation and Gender Insubordination." *The Gay and Lesbian Studies Reader*. Ed. H. Abelove, M. Barale, and D. Halperin. NY: Routledge, 1993: 307-320.

_____. *Undoing Gender*. NY: Routledge, 2004.

Carroll, Lewis. *Through the Looking-Glass. The Complete Illustrated Works of Lewis Carroll*. Ed. Edward Giuliano. NY: Avenel, 1982.

Case, Sue-Ellen. "Toward a Butch-Femme Aesthetic." *The Lesbian and Gay Studies Reader*. Ed. H. Abelove, M. Barale, and D. Halperin. NY: Routledge, 1993: 294-306.

Eliason, Michele J. "Identity Formation for Lesbian, Bisexual, and Gay Persons: Beyond a 'Minoritizing' View." *Journal of Homosexuality* 30:3 (26 March 1996), 31-58.

Falco, K.L. "Lesbian Identity Formation." In K.L. Falco, *Psychotherapy with Lesbian Clients: Theory into Practice*. NY: Brunner/Mazel, 1991: 80-105.

Hallett, Joe. "Right-winger's Bill to Stifle Campus Left-Leaners is a Surefire Backfire." *The Columbus Dispatch*. 30 January 2005: 05C.

Herek, Gregory M., Jeanine Cooper, J. Roy Gillis, and Erik Glunt. "Correlates of Internalized Homophobia in a Community Sample of Lesbians and Gay Men." *Journal of the Gay and Lesbian Medical Association* 2 (1997), 17-25.

Jagose, Annamarie. *Queer Theory: An Introduction*. NY: New York UP, 1996.

Jeffreys, Sheila. "The Queer Disappearance of Lesbians: Sexuality in the Academy." *Women's Studies International Forum* 17:5 (1994), 459-72.

Johnston, Jill. *Lesbian Nation: The Feminist Solution*. NY: Touchstone, 1973.

Koedt, Anne. "Lesbianism and Feminism." 1971. 19 February 2005. Available at: *http://www.cwluherstory.com/CWLUArchive/lesbianfeminism.html*.

Lee, Barbara A. "Increasing the Representation of Women Full Professors in Academe." www.lige.dk/Files/images/ kvinder_i_ledelse/kil/forskning/lee.ppt. 30 January 2005.

Lewis, C.S. *The Lion, the Witch, and the Wardrobe*. NY: HarperCollins, 1978.

Madden, Ed. "Immersive Pedagogies, or 'Can You Feel It, Joe?'" *Queen: A Journal of Rhetoric and Power.* http://www.ars-rhetorica.net/Queen/VolumeSpecialIssue/Articles/EdMadden.html. 1-39. 1 February 2005.

Malinowitz, Harriet. *Textual Orientations: Lesbian and Gay Students and the Making of Discourse Communities.* Portsmouth NH: Heinemann/Boynton-Cook, 1995.

Margolies, L., M. Becker, and K. Jackson-Brewer. "Internalized Homophobia: Identifying and Treating the Oppressor Within." *Lesbian Psychologies.* Boston Lesbian Psychologies Collective, Inc., Ed. Urbana IL: U of Illinois P, 1987: 229-241.

Rowling, J.K. *Harry Potter and the Sorcerer's Stone.* NY: Scholastic, 1998.

Sullivan, Nikki. *A Critical Introduction to Queer Theory.* NY: New York UP, 2003.

Sultanoff, Steve. "What is Humor?" *Association for Applied and Therapeutic Humor.* http://www.aath.org/aath_qa.html. 6 February 2005.

Tyler, Robin. "Gay & Lesbian Freedom Riders Bus to Mississippi Destination: Ovett." http://www.qrd.org/qrd/usa/mississippi/1995/freedom.rides.to.ovett-05.26-30.95 1 February 2005.

Index

Palmer, George Herbert, 3-4
Poor, attitudes toward, 70-71
Porter, Polly, 4
Powell, Justice Lewis F., 126-127
Primus, Rebecca, 5
Privileges, unruly, 91-92
Privileges vs. rights, 99-100
Productivity, in distance relationships, 50
Promotion, discrimination in, 31

Queen's University, 95,103
Queer critique, 108-110
Queer gender camp, 121-122
Queer identity, 109-110
Queer literacy, 107,126. *See also* Transformation

Raeburn, Nicole, 29-30,33
Rape, 33
"Resisting Reasonableness" (Gallop), 102-103
Retrieving the American Past, 32
Rights vs. privileges, 99-100
Rivera, Rhonda, 34-35
Rupp, Leila, 9,25-39

Same-sex benefits, vs. spousal hiring, 93
Same-sex marriage, 97
Schneider, Beth, 37
Separation, enforced, 9-10. *See also* Distance relationships
Sexism, 114-115
Sexuality, spousal hiring and, 91-92,94
Shackford, Martha, xiii
Sherwood, Margaret, 6,xiii
Significant Others (Chadwick & de Courtivron), 18-19
Smith, Mary Kozet, 4
Social discrimination, 31-32
Soland, Birgitte, 32

Spousal hiring, 73-89
alternatives to, 100-101
in Canada, 94-98
compulsory coupledom and, 96
desirability of, 100
economy of the invisible and, 98-101
heterosexual couples and, 98
labor-force optimization argument, 96
as moral issue, 93-94
objections to, 89-105
as privilege vs. right, 91-92, 99-100
rationales for, 92-93
sexist aspects, 10,96-97
sexuality and, 91-92,94
as unofficial policy, 94-95, 96-97
vs. same-sex benefits, 93
Starr, Ellen, 4
Stein, Gertrude, 4
Stressors, in distance relationships, 44-46
Stuck, Mary Frances, 9-10,41-56
SUNY Cortland, 41-56
SUNY Oswego, 41-56
Survival in the Doldrums (Rapp & Taylor), 35

Taylor, Verta, 9,25-39
Team teaching, 10,57-73
classroom experience, 61-66
conclusion, 71
dependent variable, 59-60
independent variable, 60-63
intervening variables, 63-64
reflections on findings, 68-69
schools and courses taught, 65
student response to difference, 59-60
Tenure, discrimination in, 31
Textual Orientations (Malinowitz), 115

BOOK ORDER FORM!

Order a copy of this book with this form or online at:
http://www.haworthpress.com/store/product.asp?sku=5713

Lesbian Academic Couples

_____ in softbound at $19.95 ISBN-13: 978-1-56023-619-1 / ISBN-10: 1-56023-619-1.
_____ in hardbound at $29.95 ISBN-13: 978-1-56023-618-4 / ISBN-10: 1-56023-618-3.

COST OF BOOKS _____

POSTAGE & HANDLING _____
US: $4.00 for first book & $1.50
for each additional book.
Outside US: $5.00 for first book
& $2.00 for each additional book.

SUBTOTAL _____

In Canada: add 7% GST. _____

STATE TAX _____
CA, IL, IN, MN, NJ, NY, OH, PA & SD residents
please add appropriate local sales tax.

FINAL TOTAL _____
If paying in Canadian funds, convert
using the current exchange rate,
UNESCO coupons welcome.

❑ BILL ME LATER:
Bill-me option is good on US/Canada/
Mexico orders only; not good to jobbers,
wholesalers, or subscription agencies.

❑ **Signature** _____

❑ **Payment Enclosed: $** _____

❑ **PLEASE CHARGE TO MY CREDIT CARD:**
❑ Visa ❑ MasterCard ❑ AmEx ❑ Discover
❑ Diner's Club ❑ Eurocard ❑ JCB

Account # _____

Exp Date _____

Signature _____
(Prices in US dollars and subject to change without notice.)

PLEASE PRINT ALL INFORMATION OR ATTACH YOUR BUSINESS CARD		
Name		
Address		
City	State/Province	Zip/Postal Code
Country		
Tel	Fax	
E-Mail		

May we use your e-mail address for confirmations and other types of information? ❑ Yes ❑ No We appreciate receiving
your e-mail address. Haworth would like to e-mail special discount offers to you, as a preferred customer.
We will never share, rent, or exchange your e-mail address. We regard such actions as an invasion of your privacy.

Order from your **local bookstore** or directly from
The Haworth Press, Inc. 10 Alice Street, Binghamton, New York 13904-1580 • USA
Call our toll-free number (1-800-429-6784) / Outside US/Canada: (607) 722-5857
Fax: 1-800-895-0582 / Outside US/Canada: (607) 771-0012
E-mail your order to us: orders@haworthpress.com

For orders outside US and Canada, you may wish to order through your local
sales representative, distributor, or bookseller.
For information, see http://haworthpress.com/distributors

(Discounts are available for individual orders in US and Canada only, not booksellers/distributors.)

Please photocopy this form for your personal use.
www.HaworthPress.com

BOF06